D1737063

VIKING

THAROOROSAURUS

SHASHI THAROOR is the bestselling author of twenty books, both fiction and non-fiction, besides being a noted critic and columnist. His books include the path-breaking satire *The Great Indian Novel* (1989), the classic *India: From Midnight to the Millennium* (1997), the bestselling *An Era of Darkness: The British Empire in India*, for which he won the Ramnath Goenka Award for Excellence in Journalism, 2016, for Books (Non-Fiction), and *The Paradoxical Prime Minister: Narendra Modi and His India*. He has been Under Secretary-General of the United Nations and Minister of State for Human Resource Development and Minister of State for External Affairs in the Government of India. He is a three-time member of the Lok Sabha from Thiruvananthapuram and chairs the Parliament Information Technology committee. He has won numerous literary awards, including a national Sahitya Akademi award, a Commonwealth Writers' Prize and the Crossword Lifetime Achievement Award. He was awarded the Pravasi Bharatiya Samman, India's highest honour for overseas Indians, in 2004, and honoured as New Age Politician of the Year (2010) by NDTV.

ALSO BY SHASHI THAROOR

Non-fiction

The New World Disorder and the Indian Imperative (with Samir Saran)
The Hindu Way: An Introduction to Hinduism
The Paradoxical Prime Minister: Narendra Modi and His India
Why I Am a Hindu
An Era of Darkness: The British Empire in India
India Shastra: Reflections on the Nation in Our Time
India: The Future Is Now (ed.)
Pax Indica: India and the World of the 21st Century
Shadows across the Playing Field: 60 Years of India-Pakistan Cricket
(with Shahryar Khan)
India (with Ferrante Ferranti)
The Elephant, The Tiger, And the Cell Phone: Reflections on India in the
21st Century
Bookless in Baghdad
Nehru: The Invention of India
Kerala: God's Own Country (with M.F. Husain)
India: From Midnight to the Millennium and Beyond
Reasons of State

Fiction

Riot
The Five Dollar Smile and Other Stories
Show Business
The Great Indian Novel

THAROOROSAURUS!

SHASHI THAROOR

Illustrations by Mihir Joglekar

PENGUIN

VIKING

An imprint of Penguin Random House

VIKING

USA | Canada | UK | Ireland | Australia
New Zealand | India | South Africa | China

Viking is part of the Penguin Random House group of companies
whose addresses can be found at global.penguinrandomhouse.com

Published by Penguin Random House India Pvt. Ltd
7th Floor, Infinity Tower C, DLF Cyber City,
Gurgaon 122 002, Haryana, India

First published in Viking by Penguin Random House India 2020

Copyright © Shashi Tharoor 2020
Illustrations copyright © Mihir Joglekar 2020

ISBN 9780670092604

Book design and layout by Devangana Dash
Typeset in Baskerville by Manipal Technologies Limited, Manipal
Printed at Thomson Press India Ltd, New Delhi

www.penguin.co.in

To my father Chandran Tharoor
from whom I inherited my love of words

Contents

Preface

The title 'Tharoorosaurus' was coined by Meru Gokhale, the publisher of Penguin India, who proposed the idea for this book in the rear seat of a taxicab in Jaipur as the two of us were heading to an event of the famed literary festival there. It was her idea of pitching me a book whose title would combine my name with the words tyrannosaurus (since so many are terrified of difficult words) and thesaurus (since people want to be able to look them up). I laughed it off then, but she persisted, I began to think it might be fun to do after all, and here is the result.

This is not a scholarly book; I am neither a trained linguist nor philologist, and I have no pretensions to being a qualified English teacher either. It is rather the work of someone who loves words, has loved them all his life, and whose cherished childhood memories revolve around word games with a father who was even more obsessed with them than I am. My father instilled in me the conviction that words are what shape ideas and reflect thought, and the more words you know, the more precisely and effectively are you able to express your thoughts and ideas. In addition, he delighted in the way words could be put together, their origins and the letters of which they were made; there was no word game at which he did not excel, from Scrabble to Bingo to jumbled acrostics in the newspaper—and several guess-the-word games of his own devising that kept us busy and distracted on car journeys throughout his life. If *Tharoorosaurus* imparts to its readers some of the pleasure and delight that words have long afforded me, its purpose will have been amply served.

In 2019, I had begun a 'Word of the Week' column every Sunday in a major newspaper. These began initially as lightly-tossed-off paragraphs, of some 200 words or so, on each word chosen, but as interest grew and readers sought more, I began to take the exercise more seriously, turning out 500–800-word columns instead that delved into the etymology of each word and came up with anecdotes about its usage, literary citations and nuggets of history. This book uses the latter format, so that most of the short essays in this book have not appeared anywhere else in this form.

The original idea was to publish fifty pieces in this volume; inspired by my weekly column, I suggested fifty-two, one for each week of the year, in the hope that people would dip into it and keep going back for more. In the end, this volume includes short essays on fifty-three words, since the book is being published in a leap year and we thought we may as well add an extra word for the extra leap day!

A profound word of thanks to Prof. Sheeba Thattil, without whose tireless research, creative thinking and timely assistance, this book would not have been possible. My thanks, too, to the *Hindustan Times*, for whom I first began to explore many of these words. Though this volume stands by itself, independent of the columns, I am grateful to the *Hindustan Times*, and in particular Poonam Saxena and Poulomi Banerjee, for setting me off on this journey.

Shashi Tharoor
March 2020

1.
Agathokakological

adjective

CONSISTING OF BOTH GOOD AND EVIL

———

USAGE

The Mahabharata is unusual among the great epics because its heroes are not perfect idealized figures, but agathokakological human beings with desires and ambitions who are prone to lust, greed and anger and capable of deceit, jealousy and unfairness.

Let's face it, ours is an agathokakological world, and who knows that better than Indians? We live in an era devoid of perfect heroes, where some who are hailed with passionate admiration are despised with equal intensity by others. Nothing around us seems all good or all bad. Indian philosophical systems have always had room for the theory that two opposite poles of good and evil that are considered contradictory can yet coexist naturally in a person, place, or time.

The perfect word to summarize that is agathokakological, which seems to have been coined in the early nineteenth century by sometime British Poet Laureate Robert Southey, best known for his ballad 'The Inchcape Rock', which tells the story of a fourteenth-century attempt by the Abbot of Aberbrothock to install a warning bell on a sandstone reef called Inchcape (I studied the blessed poem in Mumbai in Class 6, which is when I first heard of Southey). So the word precedes Agatha Christie, whose villainous narrators and seemingly innocent murders are not the inspiration for the term. Southey appears to have combined the Greek roots *agath-*(good), *kako-*(a variant of *cac-*, meaning bad), and *−logical* (which comes from *logos*, meaning word).

Southey was particularly prone to coining new words, or neologisms; the *Oxford English Dictionary* cites him as the earliest known author for almost 400 words. Unfortunately for him, very few of his coinages ever caught on, and agathokakological is not exactly in wide use either. The fact is that most of Southey's compound words were on the hefty side, and few filled as much of a gap in the language as this one arguably does. After all, do we really need other Southey inventions like futilitarian (a person devoted to futility) or batrachophagous (frog-eating), which he came up with? One word which might just see a revival, though, is epistolization (writing in the form of a letter): as abbreviations, acronyms and emojis become substitutes for real words, may we dare hope for the epistolization of emails?

2.
Apostrophe

noun

A PUNCTUATION MARK INDICATING
AN OMITTED LETTER (')

The closing of the Apostrophe Protection Society
because of the 'ignorance and laziness' of the
general public strikes a body blow against those
fighting for correct English.

This entry is prompted by the news that, after eighteen years of existence, the British Apostrophe Protection Society has been disbanded by its founder and chairman, retired journalist John Richards, because, in his words, 'the ignorance and laziness present in modern times have won!' Despite his best efforts, he told the media, he lost the battle for proper usage of the 'much abused' apostrophe. The apostrophe was introduced into English in the sixteenth century in imitation of French practice; but just as English has dropped the various accent marks that still abound in French, some feel the apostrophe should be dispensed with as superfluous and unnecessary.

This humble punctuation mark is more often misunderstood and misused than any other. Derived from the late Latin *apostrophus* and the Greek *apostrophos*, signifying turning away, it first referred to an orator turning aside in the course of a speech to address someone briefly before returning to his audience. But now it stands for a mark showing where a letter has been omitted in a word. In English, the mark often stands in for 'I', as in 'it's' for 'it is', or indicates possession ('Modi's government'), or marks contractions ('I'll', rather than 'I will', or ''twas' for 'it was'). Sometimes, more disputably, it's used for abbreviations, as in T'puram for Thiruvananthapuram, or to indicate the plurals of numbers ('three 7's'), letters ('there are four s's and two p's in Mississippi'), symbols ('too many &'s and #'s'), acronyms ('mind your p's and q's') or decadal dates ('he was stoned through most of the'70's'). Another distinct function of the apostrophe is disambiguation (to make your meaning clear); more on this later.

However, as grammarians and rhetoricians will tell you, that is not all. We apostrophize when we address or appeal to someone who is not present: 'Oh Mahatma Gandhi, where are you now when we really need you?' That too is called an apostrophe. But unless you are given to such overly dramatic flourishes, this form of apostrophe need not detain us much here.

The apostrophe as a punctuation mark, however, poses ordinary users of English a number of problems. The most common is people's tendency to use 'it's' when they mean 'its'—a confusion arising, no doubt, from the assumption that the apostrophe is needed to indicate possession (but 'its' is that curse of all grammar students, an exception). Also on the list of challenges would be when the possessive use of the apostrophe involves a double s, as in 'Jesus's disciples'. Many prefer to leave the second s out altogether, and let the apostrophe do double duty in standing for both a possessive and an omitted letter, writing 'Jesus' disciples'. Other exceptions are generally made for familiar phrases like whys and wherefores, oohs and ahs, ins and outs.

Life gets really complicated when you're dealing with a phrase like 'do's and don'ts'. The *Oxford Style Guide* suggests spelling it as 'dos and don'ts', which looks odd and inconsistent—and Lynne Truss, author of the delightful book on punctuation, *Eats, Shoots & Leaves*, argues for 'do's and don't's'. So there's no unanimity on the do's and don'ts of apostrophizing.

A simple trick is to remember the exceptions: it's is always 'it is', 'who's' is always 'who is', and the possessive forms are 'its' and 'whose'. Another is 'won't', which is not a contraction of 'will not' (then it would have to be 'wi'n't') but of the archaic 'woll not', which means the same thing.

One clear rule of thumb could be to use apostrophes when not using them would obscure your meaning or even confuse your reader. For example, the phrase 'dot your i's and cross your t's'. If you left out the apostrophe, it would become 'dot your is and cross your ts'. Since 'is' is a different word altogether, omitting the apostrophe would require your reader to pause and reread the sentence to get the intended meaning. The rule of disambiguation makes it clear that if an apostrophe will avoid confusion, you should use it.

The usefulness of the apostrophe was made clear when the British novelist Kingsley Amis, challenged to produce a sentence whose meaning depended on a possessive apostrophe, came up with three versions of the same sentence:

'Those things over there are my husband's.'
(*Those things over there belong to my husband.*)

'Those things over there are my husbands'.'
(*Those things over there belong to several husbands of mine.*)

'Those things over there are my husbands.'
(*I'm married to those men over there, who are just things to me.*)

On the other hand, when it's not needed, don't use it. The British speak ruefully of the 'greengrocer's apostrophe', an error made particularly in signs on grocery stores saying 'banana's by the dozen', 'carrot's for sale', and so unnecessarily on. But what can one do about the retail trade when chains have inflicted such howlers on the world as 'Toys "R" Us' and other examples of punctuation as decoration?

Opponents of the apostrophe have pointed to the maddening inconsistency of its use in everyday life. Take just one common name found in many British cities. While Newcastle United play football at a stadium called St James' Park, Exeter City play at St James Park (no apostrophe), and London has a St James's Park (apostrophe plus second s), though it really is a park and not a football stadium!

Many have suggested that apostrophes ought to be abandoned altogether, as the department store Harrods has done, but the grocery chain Sainsbury's have refused to. The argument is that they are superfluous, and the meaning is evident to most people with or without it. This 'apostrophe apostasy' is not new: George Bernard Shaw called them 'uncouth bacilli', and many linguists have argued that apostrophes are unnecessary. They may have begun to go out of fashion, as the Apostrophe Society has concluded, but let's use them till the cry goes out: 'it's time's up for the apostrophe!'

3.
Aptagram

noun

AN ANAGRAM THAT INCORPORATES
THE MEANING OF A WORD

USAGE

She loved coining aptagrams as a hobby, chuckling as she
transformed 'astronomer' into 'moon starer'.

The word aptagram is a neologism, coined near the end of the twentieth century from a combination of the Latin word *aptus*, meaning connected, and the English word 'anagram'. Creating an aptagram is a fun way of fooling around with words, but there's surely a limit to how many meaningful coinages you can come up with that both make sense and retain the original sense of the word you are breaking up. The trick is to rearrange the letters of the word into another word or phrase that conveys a related idea or even, as with 'moon starer', define the word (in this case, 'astronomer') that you are turning into an aptagram. You have to use every letter in the one word to create the other for it to qualify as an aptagram. 'Tones' and 'notes' (in the musical sense) are aptagrams of each other. So are 'angered' and 'enraged'. One clever phrase I came across turns 'laptop machines' into 'Apple Macintosh'.

The most famously historic aptagram isn't in English, but in Latin. In a biblical passage, Pontius Pilate asks Jesus 'what is truth?'—or in Latin, *'quid est veritas?'* Jesus responds with an aptagram of the question: *'est vir qui adest'*, meaning 'it is the man who is here'. Brilliant, even if, tragically, it didn't save Him from the Cross.

Some aptagrams can be pretty witty: only a parent could have converted 'dormitory' into 'dirty room' and only an exhausted salesman would think of 'customers' as 'store scum'. A conservative would convert 'revolution' into 'love to ruin'. An irritated freelancer might have changed 'editor' to 'redo it', which editors often ask you to do, and 'irritated' itself becomes 'rat, I tried', which is guaranteed to offend most editors.

Some come close, but not quite: 'the evil eyes' can become 'vile, they see', but there's something artificial about the aptagram. Changing 'dictionary' to 'indicatory' isn't grammatical enough to qualify, and 'laudatory' to 'adulatory' seems too obvious to elicit any applause. 'Lotus louts' might be anagrams for BJP-affiliated rowdies, but not aptagrams, since 'lotus' and 'louts' don't always connote the same thing!

Some aptagrams are clever but don't quite work: 'schoolmaster' doesn't really mean 'the classroom', though both use up the same set of letters. (On the other hand, if the schoolmaster gives an errant pupil 'nine thumps' in the classroom, that could be aptagrammed into 'punishment'!)

The animated television series *The Simpsons* had a character who created aptagrams out of famous people's names that described them well—thus 'Alec Guinness' became 'genuine class'. Not long ago, BJP supporters put it out that, following this rule, 'Narendra Modi' was 'a Rare Diamond'. They were quickly corrected by language mavens who pointed out that the prime minister's name contained an extra N and the correct aptagram would be 'Rare Diamond? Na!' Political opponents of the PM leapt at the opportunity to come up with 'a modern drain' and 'a modern nadir'. The nastier ones wrote, 'Married and No!' The PM's fondness for the Indian diaspora led to suggestions of 'Adore Damn NRI' and 'Dear Nomad NRI'. Of course, his supporters also hit back with 'Dream and Iron' as the qualities he represents to the nation.

The Harry Potter series has a character called Tom Marvolo Riddle whose name is an aptagram of 'I am Lord Voldemort', the series' villain. This 'inside joke' is a key part of one book's storyline, but with the Harry Potter books being translated into sixty-eight languages, publishers around the world were forced to devise ingenious apatagrams that would mean the same thing. They found the solution in changing the name of the character to something that could be aptagrammed into 'I am Lord Voldemort' in their own language. (So in French, for instance, Tom Marvolo Riddle becomes Tom Elvis Jedusor, so that his name is still an aptagram of 'Je Suis Voldemort'.) This worked in all the Romance languages, which changed the character's names into various aptagrams of the phrase 'I am Lord Voldemort' in their own languages—but when it came to Chinese, which uses characters and not letters, the translator was stumped. The publisher had to resort to a footnote to explain that English has something called aptagrams!

The cleverest aptagram of all, perhaps, is transforming 'eleven plus two' to 'twelve plus one', which apart from using all the letters, is also mathematically accurate. The more you try, however, the more contrived the exercise becomes ('brush' as 'shrub', for instance) which is why aptagrams haven't widely caught on. It could still work as a party game for bored English 'teachers', who could become 'cheaters' by using the Internet to do their work for them!

4.
Authorism

noun

A WORD, PHRASE OR NAME CREATED BY AN
AUTHOR, WHICH PASSES INTO COMMON USAGE

———

USAGE

The works of Shakespeare include hundreds of
authorisms, including words now commonly used but
unheard before his time, like 'bump', 'hurry' and 'critical'.

Authorism is actually a neologism, a new word coinage. It was invented—or at least first used in this sense—by the language scholar Paul Dickson for the express purpose of giving a name to his book on words invented by authors, *Authorisms: Words Wrought by Writers*, published in 2014 on the occasion of William Shakespeare's 450th birthday. (The word had been used in the past to relate to the state of being a writer, as when Horace Walpole, in the late eighteenth century, discussed a writer too satisfied with his 'authorism'.)

Shakespeare was the uncrowned king of authorisms. His written vocabulary, Dickson tells us, consisted of 17,245 words, many of which he simply made up for his plays. These included terms that are so essential to our everyday conversation—like 'bump', 'road', 'hurry', 'critical' and 'bedazzled'—that one wonders how English coped without them before Shakespeare dreamt them up. Scholars have tripped over each other in the effort to count Shakespeare's authorisms: some put the total at 500, others come up with the extraordinary number of 1700. Aside from individual words,

Shakespeare's authorisms include famous phrases that have come into common use since his day, like 'brave new world', 'all's well that ends well', 'setting your teeth on edge' and 'being cruel only to be kind'. No wonder George Bernard Shaw created an authorism to describe excessive worship of Shakespeare: bardolatry.

If Shakespeare coined the most authorisms, the poet John Milton offers the most competition, with this tally clocking in at 630 new words, including such familiar words and phrases as 'earth-shaking', 'lovelorn', 'fragrance', 'by hook or crook' and 'pandemonium'. Mind you, not everything Milton came up with stood the test of time, or that of necessity: few later generations found much use for many of Milton's authorisms such as 'ensanguined', 'emblazonry' and 'horrent'!

The early litterateurs had the opportunity to establish themselves in a language that was still growing. Geoffrey Chaucer, Ben Jonson, John Donne and Sir Thomas Moore also are credited with several authorisms each. Chaucer gave the English such essentials as 'bagpipe' and 'universe', while Moore contributed 'anticipate' and 'fact'. Ben Johnson is said to have invented 558 words, John Donne 342. English grew beautifully in their care.

Later writers had to contend with the fact that so many words had already been invented that there was less need for neologisms. Still, Charles Dickens came up with many original terms and phrases, gleaned, it is suggested, from expressions he had heard around the poorer quarters and criminal classes of London. Mark Twain, Dickson tells us, didn't take credit for any authorisms at all, but did claim that he popularized the language of the Mississippi River and words derived from the Gold Rushes of Nevada and California (for example, 'hardpan', 'strike it rich' and 'bonanza'). It is said that Twain's talent for creative usage gave new meanings to existing words—like 'hard-boiled', which he is credited for turning into a synonym for 'tough'.

By the twentieth century one would imagine the scope for totally new authorisms declined. The popular American writer Sinclair Lewis tried hard to create authorisms that might stick, but none of his invented words—from 'Kiplingo' for Rudyard's bombastic prose to 'teetotalitarian' for advocates of Prohibition to 'philanthrobber' for a robber baron who dabbled in philanthropy—passed into popular usage, let alone endured. George Orwell's 1984 (a date derived from reversing the last two digits of the year it was written, 1948) takes the prize, though, for imparting chilling new meanings to commonly used words and combining some ordinary words into sinister new phrases. These ranged from 'Big Brother' as a term to describe a totalitarian dictator, to the more specific 'doublethink' and 'newspeak' which anticipate the 'post-truth' and 'fake news' of our times.

5.
Brickbat

noun

AN UNFAVOURABLE CRITICISM,
UNKIND REMARK OR SHARP PUT-DOWN

USAGE

The politician's performance in his constituency merited
the several brickbats thrown at him by his critics.

As one can imagine, the word 'brickbat' began its innings literally rather than metaphorically in the mid-sixteenth century, describing a piece of brick (half a brick or less, but always, according to purists, retaining one unbroken end of the brick) used as a handy projectile, especially where stones were scarce, to throw at people one disapproved of. The word comes, of course, from the words brick and bat, the latter in the sense of a lump, or a piece (I know we think of a bat as a club we wield in cricket, but the 'lump' meaning still exists, as in the lumps of cotton wadding used in quilts that are still called 'batting').

Soon enough the literal sense gave way to the figurative, so that rather than using a brickbat as a missile, it began to refer to comments, insults, and the like. By 1642, the poet John Milton was using the word in a figurative sense to mean an uncomplimentary remark or a harsh criticism ('I beseech ye friends, ere the brick-bats flye, resolve me and yourselves . . .'). Literary and theatre critics are particularly fond of flinging brickbats at the works and writers they don't think highly of, and doing so literally might land them in jail, so brickbat-as-metaphor is the usage we usually come across.

In this sense a brickbat is more nasty than a mere negative word; its use implies an insult hurled at a target with an intent to wound, and therefore can only be applied to extremely blunt criticism. It is often mated with its contrasting opposite, 'bouquet'—as in, 'Poor Shashi Tharoor has both bouquets and brickbats showered on his head daily for anything he says!' This is a twentieth-century usage that may have faded with that century, because one comes across the pair far less often than one sees brickbats flying by themselves. Perhaps we are just an unkinder species now!

Some of you will recall the adage 'bricks and stones may break my bones, but words can never hurt me'. Whoever said that, and the many who thought it wise enough to pass it down over the generations as a proverb worth citing, needs to have a brickbat thrown at them. A broken bone heals far more quickly and durably than the emotional and psychic injuries inflicted by a savage word, which is where the brickbat derives its power. The many libel and defamation suits that litter the courts show that the figurative brickbat hurts just as much as, if not more than, the literal one. The pen may or may not be mightier than the sword, but it can indeed be as painful and offensive a weapon as the brickbat.

6.
Claque

noun

A GROUP OF PEOPLE HIRED TO APPLAUD

USAGE

No one thought much of his speech, except
the usual claque of party hacks who applauded
his every line vigorously.

With the general elections mercifully behind us, we will have fewer political speeches, less bombastic rhetoric and (one hopes) less abuse of historical figures to deal with in our daily lives and dominating our news media. But it's also time to wonder why so much of such arrant nonsense is regularly spouted by political leaders with such scant regard for the effect their words have on normal people. If they realized how they sounded to people with average sensibility and decency, surely they wouldn't speak like this?

Ah, but you're forgetting—it's not normal people they are addressing their offensive words to; it's the claques that constitute the echo chambers for their invective. Every political party has them, but some have more claques than others because they can afford to pay more for the rent-a-crowd audiences their leaders need to feel encouraged and emboldened by.

The word itself goes back to the mid-nineteenth century, and comes from the French expression *claqueurs*, a band of men hired by a theatre management and distributed through the audience in the hall to applaud the performance of the actors. This method of helping ensure the success of public performances is pretty old; it is said that the Roman Emperor Nero fancied himself a bit of a thespian, and whenever he acted, ensured that 5000 of his paid soldiers were on hand to lead a thunderous ovation for his performances. But it seems to have really become an organized system, set up and controlled by the claqueurs themselves, in Paris in the early years of the nineteenth century, when an agency was set up in that city in 1820 by a Mr Sauton to manage and supply claqueurs.

Since the word is derived from the verb *claquer*, meaning 'to clap', the term leaves no doubt about the principal task of the profession. Claque members received money and free tickets to the early performances of plays, opera performances and the like; they were instructed to laugh, cry, shout and, of course, clap at just the right moments, with a view to setting an example for the rest of the audience, and in the hope of igniting similar responses and influencing them to do the same.

The practice began to die out by the early twentieth century, not least because claques became expert at extortion, threatening to boo instead of clap if they were not paid more. The transition from theatre to politics is more metaphorical than literal: few politicians can actually afford to pay a claque just to applaud them. But the tribe of hangers-on that politicians maintain with a variety of incentives (party positions, minor government offices, titles, sometimes pay) are happy to play the role of the old claqueurs when required.

Surrounded by cliques and applauded by claques, no wonder so many of our political leaders are so out of touch with reality—and with the public they claim to represent.

7.
Contronym

noun

A WORD THAT CAN ALSO MEAN THE OPPOSITE
OF ITSELF, A FEATURE MORE COMMON IN
ENGLISH THAN IN ANY INDIAN LANGUAGE

USAGE

When the media said President Trump had sanctioned
Iranian oil supplies, I wasn't sure what they meant, since
'sanction' is a contronym.

In this instance, confusion is understandable, because the headline could mean the president had *permitted* the oil supplies to flow, or that he had *prohibited* them. If you get a sanction from an authority to do something, it means the former; but if you impose sanctions on someone or something, it means the latter. The word 'sanction' can either refer to approval for a course of action or a penalty for disobeying an injunction. That's why it's a contronym, also sometimes known as a 'Janus word' (after the Roman God with two faces).

Confused? 'Sanction' is not the only case of a word that can be used to mean its own opposite. We use contronyms all the time without realizing it; the most common contronym might be the word 'off', since 'setting off' an alarm activates a warning bell, while 'switching off' the alarm deactivates it—and both use the same 'off'. If you find too many objects gathering dust at home, you can tell your maid that she needs to dust more so there is less dust (that's not a contradiction, just a contronym!) Similarly, strike can be used to mean to create (as in 'strike a deal') or to eliminate ('strike that line from the record'). And if you say you have 'finished' something, is it completed or destroyed?

A puppy can leap at a target with a single 'bound', but if it's 'bound' to a post, it is restrained and restricted. When you go fast, you are moving rapidly, but when you hold fast, you are unmoving and unmoved. If you have a 'handicap', it's a disadvantage that impedes you; but in many sports, especially golf, a handicap is an advantage. At a party you can be told there are 'just a few dishes left', which means they remain to be consumed, while some people have left, which means they've gone. 'Left' is even more complicated because of its political meaning—a person from the left can be sitting on the right (and vice-versa!)

When the United Nations created an in-house inspectorate and named the department the Office of Internal Oversight Services, I warned my colleagues, only half in jest, that every time the new office messed up, they could say, 'Hey, it was just an oversight.' Oversight is also a contronym: it can mean watchful supervision, but also an inadvertent error. Similarly, the word cleave can mean both 'to cut apart' ('the warrior cleaved his enemy's head from his neck') or 'to bind together' ('the infant cleaved to his mother's bosom'). So can 'clip' mean to cut something (as in a newspaper clipping) or to hold them together ('Can you clip those clippings together please?') A criminal might 'bolt' (meaning he runs away or 'exits quickly') but you can bolt the door shut (meaning fix it in place to immobilize it).

There are contronyms that demonstrate the truth of the adage that America and Britain are two countries divided by a common language. For example, 'table'—to table a bill means 'to put it up for debate' in British English, while if you table a bill in the US Congress, it means 'to remove it from debate'. A 'moot' point is one that requires discussion and debate in Britain, whereas in America, if an issue is moot, it is dead and unnecessary to discuss.

American usage multiplies the range of contronyms. A 'hold-up', in the US, can either support or impede: wooden beams might hold up the ceiling, but a mugger might trap you in a hold-up at gunpoint (or traffic can create a hold-up on the road).

Also in America, you can use bills to pay bills (what we call 'notes' are 'bills' in the US, so 'dollar bills' can be used to settle your restaurant bills!).

'Variety' can mean a particular type ('Alphonso? That's a great variety of mango you're eating') or many types ('India grows a variety of mangoes'). You can 'execute' a plan to carry it out, but if you execute the planner, you are terminating him. If you 'buckle' your belt or a horse's saddle, you fasten it; but if your knees buckle, you are about to collapse. 'Give out' is our final example: a charity can give out aid to flood victims, or an exhausted victim fleeing the floods can collapse when his legs give out.

My space has just given out, so I'll call it a day. That's perhaps the most common contronym of all—you usually call it a day when it's night!

8.
Cromulent
adjective

APPEARING LEGITIMATE BUT ACTUALLY BEING
SPURIOUS

USAGE

The government's statement to the Supreme Court on the
migrant workers' crisis made a cromulent case, based on
the argument that no migrant worker had perished on the
way home—which in fact turned out not to be the case, as
media reports of their travails flowed in.

As we all know, the Supreme Court came in for a lot of flak from lawyers for taking the solicitor-general's word on the issue of the migrant workers. It was only some weeks later that, in the face of widespread criticism, the court instructed the government to transport all the migrant workers home within fifteen days. But initially the Supreme Court was taken in by the government's cromulence.

In fact, 'cromulent' is an apposite term for much of the Modi government's claims. An administration that has spent Rs 5600 crores of taxpayers' money in its first five years on advertisements and publicity praising itself, is particularly prone to cromulence. Thus, the government boasted of creating millions of 'Jan Dhan' accounts at a time when 93 per cent of them had zero balance, and spent crores publicizing the free gas cylinders provided to poor rural women for cooking without acknowledging that the refills had to be paid for—and 97 per cent of the beneficiaries declined to do so because they could not afford the cost of a gas cylinder.

Interestingly, cromulent is a recent entrant into the English language, having first appeared, it seems, in a 1996 American television show, *The Simpsons*. From there it made its way into a US Supreme Court amicus curiae's brief, and eventually into the Merriam-Webster dictionary. Initially, it meant just 'fine' or 'acceptable', as when a character in *The Simpsons* uses the wrong term 'embiggens' instead of 'enlarges', but a teacher says 'it's a perfectly cromulent word'. That usage led to the ironic meaning the word now has, since cromulent was a fake word invented to defend the credibility of another invented word. So, something is cromulent when it sounds plausible but is actually not true or accurate.

Cromulent is not to be confused with 'crapulent', which refers to excessive drinking of alcohol, though of course a crapulent spokesperson is quite likely to make cromulent claims. Our abstemious politicians do not even have the excuse of crapulence to justify their cromulence.

9.
Curfew

noun

AN ORDER SPECIFYING A TIME DURING WHICH CERTAIN REGULATIONS APPLY, ESPECIALLY THE TIME WHEN INDIVIDUALS ARE REQUIRED TO RETURN TO AND STAY IN THEIR HOMES

———

USAGE

During the first few days of curfew, the city looked like a ghost town after 7 p.m.

//45

The word curfew has an interesting history. Literally, the word means to 'cover fire'. In the early fourteenth century, spelt *curfeu*, it meant an evening signal, involving the ringing of a bell at a fixed hour, usually 8 p.m., as a signal to extinguish fires and lights. The word curfew also denoted a cover for a fire, made of metal and designed to enclose the embers at the end of the day so that the fire could be relit easily the following morning. The curfew bell was a bell rung in the evening in medieval England as the signal for everyone to go to bed.

It was William the Conqueror in England who decreed after 1068 that all lights and fires should be covered at the ringing of an eight o'clock bell to prevent the risk of fire within the wooden timber buildings of that era. His intention may not have been purely innocent, however: the curfew was also initially used as a repressive measure to prevent rebellious meetings of the conquered Anglo-Saxons. Historians speculate that William prohibited the use of live fires after the curfew bell was rung to prevent associations and conspiracies against Norman rule by the English. But the practice long outlived that purpose. In Macaulay's history of Claybrook, *Claybrooke Magna* (1791), he says, 'The custom of ringing curfew, which is still kept up in Claybrook, has probably obtained without intermission since the days of the Norman Conqueror.'

Today a curfew is an order issued by the public authorities or military forces requiring everyone or certain people to be indoors at certain times, usually at night. It can be imposed to maintain public order, or suppress restive populations: a dusk-to-dawn curfew is a typical imposition by military rulers, with a shoot-at-sight order for violators. Curfews have also been imposed by the head of a household on those living in the household, as most teenagers know, since they are often required to return home by a specific time of the evening or night. College authorities rarely use the word curfew for their regulations, but most college hostels impose a daily requirement for guests to return to their hostel by a certain hour. In the UK, those who frequent pubs have their own curfew, after which patrons of licensed premises may not enter; thus 'last orders' have to be taken by a specified curfew time, usually midnight. In American League baseball, there was a 'curfew rule' under which play could not continue past 1 a.m.

In India, Section 144 of the Criminal Procedure Code (CrPC) empowers an executive magistrate to prohibit an assembly of more than four persons in an area. In about 1861, Officer Raj-Ratna E.F. Deboo used the curfew along with Section 144 to reduce overall crime in that time in the state of Baroda, an achievement for which he was awarded a gold medal by the Maharaja Gaekwad of Baroda.

Curfews are frequently imposed in riot-stricken areas but are usually a temporary measure and lifted when calm and public order are restored. Curfews have, however, been resorted to more often in Kashmir, often confining the population to a form of collective house arrest for days together in periods of heightened militancy.

More recently, of course, the prolonged lockdown prompted by the COVID-19 pandemic involved all-day curfews, obliging people to stay indoors to avoid infection. As with law-and-order curfews, these were also initially enforced by the long arm of the law, aided by lathis.

Terrorists, in turn, have imposed their own curfews, forcing shopkeepers to down their shutters and traffic to stay off the streets as a form of enforced non-cooperation with the authorities. In this instance, a curfew becomes a form of coerced protest, and the authorities, who usually enforce curfews, have to resort to inducements to keep normal activities going. Wonder what William the Conqueror would have done if the English had tried to turn the tables on him that way!

10.
Cwtch

noun

A HUG, BUT MUCH MORE
INTIMATE THAN A HUG

———

USAGE

Once the election results are out, many a defeated
candidate will be in need of a cwtch.

Derived from Welsh and pronounced 'kwootch' (almost like a sneeze that stifles a cough), cwtch features as a legitimate word in the authoritative *Oxford English Dictionary*. The Welsh have been famous for various unusual words, including the longest train station name in the world (Llanfairpwllgwyngyllgogerychwyrndrobwllllantysiliogogogoch). But the short and simple one-syllable 'cwtch', arguably, is the most special of them all.

The *Urban Dictionary* says that cwtch connotes snuggling, cuddling, loving, protecting, safeguarding and claiming, all at once. Welsh people say a cwtch is a hug that makes you feel safe, warm and comforted. (There's a second, lesser-known usage too, for a small cubbyhole in which to store things safely, but that really reinforces the metaphorical meaning.) Kate Leaver of the BBC writes of an 'emotional embrace . . . that evokes a sense of home'. She quotes a Welsh source as saying: 'A cwtch is something you do when you're overflowing with joy and love at another person's sheer existence in your life that you can't help but try and squeeze that love into them; it's a safe space of love and comfort for someone who needs it; it's all the best parts of being alive and loving someone, in a pair of arms. Hugs are for everyone; cwtches are only for a few, very special people in my life.'

Friends tell me you give a cwtch only to someone you have some close claim on; it is a sincere act, not a routine ritual like the PM's hugs of startled world leaders. It requires a culture where the giving and receiving of profound affection is normal and not hemmed in by civilities or protocol; giving a cwtch assumes a way of life and a state of mind that don't exist in every society. Strong, sincere and heartfelt affection is required for a mere hug to qualify as a cwtch. Elizabeth Taylor famously said about Richard Burton, whom she married twice (and who was Welsh), 'I just want to go and cwtch him.'

An Australian writer of Welsh origin, Chloe Sargeant, expressed it beautifully: 'When someone gives you a cwtch, you feel loved and secure and wholly shielded. . . . You feel a hug physically, but you feel a cwtch mentally, emotionally, with every fibre of your being and essence.'

The friend who introduced me to the word sent me a poem that sums it up so beautifully I can't improve upon it:

A cwtch is a Welsh word steeped in history;
From where it came is still a mystery.
It's hard to describe the feeling you get
But your first real cwtch you'll never forget.
A cwtch is wondrous morning or night.
It's always the best way to get over a fight.
As a reliever of pain it's better than pills;
It'll help you forget all of your ills.
A cwtch is a drug, addictive for sure;
Indulge in it once—you'll hunger for more.
It's more than a hug; it's more than a cuddle;
It's something you give to someone who's special.

The art of cwtching has passed down through life
From parents and lovers, from a husband or wife;
The one thing for sure that I've learned is true
The spirit of cwtching lives on in you!

11.
Defenestrate

verb

LITERALLY, TO THROW OUT OF THE WINDOW;
METAPHORICALLY, TO JETTISON

USAGE

The Opposition is united in its determination to
defenestrate the Modi government.

'Defenestrate' is one of those words one learned to use in college debates at St. Stephen's in the 1970s, combining just the right doses of gravitas and jocularity so beloved of adolescents. It was never enough to throw out something you disliked; you had to defenestrate it. Derived from the Latin word *fenestra* or 'window,' which survives in French as *fenêtre*, defenestration actually happened most famously in European history, when two Catholic deputies to the Bohemian national assembly and a secretary were tossed out of the window of the castle of Hradschin in Prague on 21 May 1618 by Protestant radicals protesting infringements of their religious freedom by regents of the Catholic Emperor Ferdinand II.

This incident, which has gone down in the history books as the 'Defenestration of Prague', had a semi-happy ending: the victims survived, but only because they landed in a pile of garbage. Their defenestration marked the start of the Thirty Years' War.

The good people of Prague had a demonstrated taste for this means of resolving their political differences. Two centuries earlier, in 1419, seven town officials were thrown from the windows of the Prague Town Hall, precipitating the Hussite War.

Less happy endings have occurred in other situations where defenestration was used as a means of execution. In Biblical days, for example, defenestration scaled the fate of Queen Jezebel, who, the *Second Book of Kings* says, was killed by being thrown out of a high window by her own eunuch servants, on the orders of Jehu. King John is said to have killed his nephew, Arthur of Brittany, by defenestration from the castle at Rouen, France, in 1203.

Closer to home (and to our own times), is the story of how Adham Khan, Akbar's general and foster brother, was defenestrated not just once but twice for murdering a rival general, Ataga Khan, a favourite of Akbar's, who had been recently promoted by Akbar. Akbar was woken up by the tumult after the murder. He struck Adham Khan down personally with his fist and immediately ordered his defenestration. The first time, his legs were broken as a result of the twelve-metre fall from the ramparts of Agra Fort, but Adham Khan survived. Akbar, in a rare act of cruelty probably reflecting his anger at the loss of his favourite general, ordered Adham Khan's defenestration a second time. This time the fall from a higher window killed him. Adham Khan's mother Maham Anga had been Akbar's wet nurse, so Akbar personally informed her of her son's death by his orders. The story goes that she dutifully replied, 'You have done well,' only to pass away of acute depression forty days later.

While the act of defenestration connotes the forcible or peremptory removal of an adversary, there is also a neutral meaning for the root word. Architects speak of a building's *fenestration*, by which they mean the style and placement of its window openings. Defenestration in this context would involve the closure or boarding-up of a building's windows.

These days, defenestrations are more metaphorical, and involve electorates jettisoning their political leaders. Few are likely to result in anything like a Thirty Years' War. The defenestration that the Indian Opposition is striving for seeks merely to end a shorter torment.

And the word lends itself to humorous use in the computer era: some say they are 'defenestrating their computer' when they describe the act of deleting Microsoft Windows as their operating system!

12.
Epicaricacy

noun

DERIVING PLEASURE FROM
THE MISFORTUNES OF OTHERS

———

USAGE

When the boastful braggart was defenestrated by his club,
my epicaricacy knew no bounds.

There's always a particular malicious satisfaction that some people gain from seeing others—especially those to whose vainglory we have been subject—receiving their comeuppance. The Germans popularized the term *schadenfreude*, but the English version of the same idea is derived from Greek, not German— it's from the Greek word *epikhairekakía*, 'joy upon evil', made up of *epi*, upon, plus *chara*, joy, and *kakon*, evil. Epicaricacy is what you feel when you chortle on hearing something bad has happened to someone else.

It's usually malicious: an article in *The Guardian* discussed the motives of internet trolls who prey on women with abuse and threats, and defined their epicaricacy as 'derivation of pleasure from the misfortunes of others'. Another citation I came across speaks of 'taking sadistic joy in the misfortune of others', involving *delectatio morose* (Italian for much the same thing). All round, epicaricacy would have to be summed up as Not Nice.

Sadly, however, all too many people seem to enjoy the humiliation and degradation of other human beings. Many of our television channels relish inflicting such humiliation upon their targets; no tragedy is too painful to be exploited by the more callous and voyeuristic of our anchors and so-called journalists. Accusing people, savouring their setbacks, degrading people who are unable to hit back, taunting others, willing others to fail, are the staple of many of our more reprehensible channels, and they have fed into, or reinforced, if they haven't actually created, a culture of relishing the downfall of others so that it makes their viewers feel better.

I'd like to think I'm largely immune from epicaricacy, because I was born without an envy gene, and have grown up convinced that the world has enough room for everyone to succeed and that the sufferings of others should never be a cause of rejoicing for myself.

Still, epicaricacy is not always evil. Arrogant braggarts need to be brought down from time to time, if only for their own good. Many a schoolchild will recall a moment of epicaricacy when a know-it-all classmate got a bad mark on a test, or the impossibly glamorous heartthrob forgot his lines during the school play, or the rich show-off lost his wallet and had to beg for tiffin money from his impecunious friends.

When these emotions get transferred to adults, however, they turn into malicious joy at others' suffering. People with low self-esteem are particularly prone to epicaricacy: the less self-esteem an individual has, the more frequently, and more intensely, will they experience epicaricacy. The joy of observing the suffering of others comes from the lesser person's feeling that failure brings the other person down, thus improving or validating their own standing and enhancing their self-worth.

Still, whether harmless or nasty, epicaricacy is to be avoided. When you smile at bad news about someone, suppress a grin and say insincerely, 'It couldn't have happened to a nicer guy,' you are experiencing epicaricacy. Grow out of it quickly, though—as any shrink will tell you, negative emotions are not good for you—or for any of us, even politicians!

13.
Epistemophilia

noun

AN EXCESSIVE LOVE OF KNOWLEDGE

———

USAGE

He was constantly nose-deep in general knowledge textbooks to a point where his epistemophilia was positively antisocial.

The term epistemophilia comes from the Greek: it's a compound of *episteme*, which means knowledge, science or understanding, and *philos*, love. Whereas epistemology is the study of the nature of knowledge, the justification and the rationality of beliefs—all of which are generally seen as good things—however, epistemophilia has a negative connotation, implying a love of knowledge that is excessive. Someone given to epistemophilia is marked by an excessive striving for or preoccupation with knowledge for its own sake.

We all know kids like that in India, mugging up useless trivia to ace quizzes, to enter 'GK' competitions and—who knows?— perhaps one day to score those extra marks in a vital competitive examination. The acquisition of knowledge is a national preoccupation in India as an end in itself, but unlike in most countries, it is rarely about acquiring true mastery of a difficult subject or deepening one's understanding of the world and its mysteries. It is rather a test of memory that involves remembering an obscure fact for its own sake and recalling it just when it matters, at the key moment when the question is asked to which that particular fact or detail is the answer.

This pursuit was a harmless enough hobby in my student days. I founded the Quiz Club in St. Stephen's College in 1974, well before 'quizzing' acquired its current monstrous proportions, and was rather proud of my mastery of trivia. But now, when every high school and college seems to be caught up in quizzing, when televised quizzes attract sponsors offering big prize money, prestige and of course fame, the culture has made epistemophilia a rampant disease in our schools and colleges. And that's decidedly not a good thing.

There's a good reason why epistemophilia is considered unhealthy and even looked down upon by many intellectuals. Knowledge is basically of two kinds, broadly defined as procedural and lexical. Procedural knowledge is the kind of knowledge that pays, since it relates to how things are done; the possessor of procedural knowledge has what used to be called 'know-how'. Lexical knowledge is a collection of facts and details on objects, properties and relations and tends to consist of memorizable information— terms, labels, titles, dates, names and so on. Scholars consider lexical knowledge to be, by definition, static and nominal; that's the kind of knowledge that describes the world rather like a fixed image, immutable and unchanging, a 'still' photo in a frozen timeframe. It's the kind of information you can easily get these days with two clicks of a mouse on Google. Lexical knowledge is therefore seen as of minor importance, and considered the lowest grade of knowledge.

Epistemophilia, alas, focuses on lexical knowledge; that's what quizzes and competitive examinations in our country largely test. It is unhealthy because it divorces knowledge from its true purpose, and because it gives its victims the wrong impression that they are knowledgeable, when all they have done is mastered information of no earthly use outside the rarefied environs of a quiz competition.

If we taught more 'procedural knowledge', the poor 'learning outcomes' coming from our schools and colleges, that educationists lament, would dramatically improve.

Here's one more campaign for our slogan-shouting campuses: 'Down With Epistemophilia!'

14.
Eponym

noun

ONE WHOSE NAME BECOMES THAT OF A PLACE,
A PEOPLE, AN ERA, OR AN INSTITUTION

USAGE

This book's eponymous author keeps protesting
that he's nothing like a dinosaur!

Eponym comes from the Greek *eponymos*, 'given as a name, giving one's name to something' as a plural noun (short for *eponymoi*, heroes) denoting founders (legendary or real) of tribes or cities. Thus, the American capital in Washington DC was never the residence of its eponymous first President, George Washington. When you speak of the Victorian era, you are referring to the period of its eponymous monarch, Queen Victoria. The Modi government is headed by its eponymous prime minister, Narendra Modi; Obamacare is a health insurance scheme named for its eponymous President, Barack Obama; Thatcherism is an economic philosophy of laissez-faire capitalism named for its strident advocate, Prime Minister Margaret Thatcher.

Eponyms are not merely useful for referring to politics. A Tudor building refers to a style made popular during the rule of its eponymous British dynasty, and a Georgian square to the eponymous King George III. 'Those Edwardian young men in spats' suggests the youth in question lived in the time of Britain's first post-Victorian monarch King Edward VII. Bowler hats, then worn by those men in spats, were invented by the eponymous William Bowler. Queen Anne furniture alludes to the eponymous British monarch of the beginning of the eighteenth century.

Common household products also refer, often unknowingly, to their eponymous creators. 'I'll Hoover it up' comes from the inventor of the vacuum-cleaner that bore his name; 'I need to fill up some diesel' takes its name from the eponymous German, Rudolf Diesel, who invented that fuel; 'let's take the kids on the Ferris wheel' credits the eponymous engineer who first came up with that enormous contraption to whirl seated people around for pleasure. If you want to hop into the jacuzzi, you are tipping your hat (or doffing your clothes) to an eponymous pair of Italian brothers. If you slip on some leotards, there's an eponymous French fashion designer, Jacques Leotard, you're memorializing. And if you eat a sandwich, you are paying tribute to the inveterate gambler, the eponymous Earl of Sandwich, who had the snack invented for him so he didn't have to interrupt his card games for a meal. When I visited Sudan in the late 1970s, it was common to hear people saying, 'I'll pick you up in my Tata,' without being conscious of the eponymous Indian vehicle manufacturer.

Thanks to Viking Penguin, I am now the eponymous author of the present volume, which derives its unusual title, as the preface explains, from my own name. I have had a similar compliment paid to me on the Internet, where a group of social media users have chosen to call themselves 'Tharoorians', describing themselves as inspired by my ideas and beliefs, which they see themselves resolutely defending against the 'trolls' (another word discussed later in this book) who oppose and attack me politically and personally.

Far more distinguished figures in our history have eponymously inspired much larger numbers of followers. The country is full of self-declared Gandhians, for instance, though few can truly be said to live up to the Mahatma's ideals and his exacting standards of personal rectitude. Another eponymous term is associated with his closest legatee. For a few decades after Independence, it was entirely reasonable to say, as a senior public figure once remarked about the entire Indian ruling class, 'we are all Nehruvians'. Today, in the face of relentless criticism from the new ruling establishment around the BJP, the Nehruvians seem to be a dwindling breed.

One 'boycotts' people throughout the English-speaking world without knowing a thing about the eponymous Captain Boycott whose unpopularity led to the term. I may as well stop here for fear of being boycotted myself . . .

15.
Farrago

noun

HODGEPODGE, A CONFUSED MIX, A JUMBLE

USAGE

The channel's accusations against me were a farrago of lies, misrepresentations and half-truths broadcast by an unprincipled showman masquerading as a journalist.

Farrago, a word that I was excessively fond of using in rebutting my debating opponents at St. Stephen's College in the early 1970s, was invented around the 1630s and came from a Latin root for 'medley, mixed fodder, mix of grains for animal feed'. It stands for a jumble, a confused mixture, and is particularly handy when refuting arguments in a debate, lending itself to frequent use in the British Parliament, for instance, in phrases like 'a farrago of excuses and obfuscation', 'a farrago of deceit and lies', 'a farrago of conspiracy theories and unproven assertion' or 'a rambling farrago of half-digested knowledge'.

The commentator Peter Bergen once dismissed a claim by the journalist Seymour Hersh as 'a farrago of nonsense that is contravened by a multitude of eyewitness accounts, inconvenient facts and simple common sense'. One stern linguist disapproved of the word's use, saying farrago 'has become one of those all-purpose dismissive words that ought to appear in public only when attached to a health warning'.

My denunciation of defamatory accusations by an Indian television channel (that I had separately characterized as the digital equivalent of a toilet roll) briefly resurrected the word's usage in India, leading to the creation of a spate of social media handles using the word.

Some of my serial abusers on Twitter even lamely took to calling me 'Mr Farrago'. But I claim no particular proprietorship of the word.

When political critics dredged up a decade-old Oxford debate of Mehdi Hasan's in which he uses the word, and accused me of stealing it from him, we both laughed; Hasan replied that neither he nor I had invented the term. A diligent reader promptly came up with a citation from a 1993 article I wrote in the *Washington Post*, and another from my 1997 book *India from Midnight to the Millennium*, which employed the word. It is true, though, that it isn't very widely used. To cite the disapproving linguist again: 'To judge from the company it keeps, it is much favoured by judges and journalists but by hardly anybody else.'

Some people, it seems, have begun using 'farrago' to mean a lot of noise and argument signifying nothing, or some happening or event which has proved a fiasco or caused a furore. That is, strictly speaking, wrong usage, though English, with its marvellous elasticity, may well evolve to accommodate this different sense of the word in due course. For now, let's just remember it whenever we are tempted to turn on our television and change to a channel that claims the nation wants to know what it should never believe.

16.

Floccinaucinihilipilification

noun

THE ACT OF ESTIMATING SOMETHING OR SOMEONE AS WORTHLESS

USAGE

My new book, *The Paradoxical Prime Minister*, is more than just a 500-page exercise in floccinaucinihilipilification.

Yes, I tweeted that, and I'll admit it was meant to grab eyeballs and draw attention to my (then) new book. I supplied the definition, too—and no, I was not making it up. But what I was not prepared for was the rage it became, as for months afterwards, parents would trot out their little four-year-old children to recite the word to me as something they had been taught to say to sound like Shashi Tharoor. Perish the thought: when I resurrected it for that tweet, I hadn't used it since college.

My favourite 'f' word (which I won't repeat throughout, since it uses up too much space to do so!) is a jocular coinage, apparently by pupils at Eton College, which combines a number of roughly synonymous Latin terms: *floccus* ('a wisp') + *naucum* ('a trifle') + *nihilum* ('nothing') + *pilus* ('a hair') + *fication*. Often considered the longest regular word in the English language, being one letter longer than the traditionally cited 'antidisestablishmentarianism', it has the merit of not referring to some obscure disease, the sin of 'pneumonoultramicroscopicsilicovolcanoconiosis', which is technically longer but impossible to use in regular conversation, since it refers to an extremely rare lung disease caused by the inhalation of ultra-fine particles. Whereas the 'f' word was even used in parliamentary debates: US Senator Jesse Helms dismissed the demise of the Comprehensive Test Ban Treaty by declaring, 'I note your distress at my floccinaucinihilipilification of the CTBT' while in the UK, Conservative MP Jacob Rees-Mogg used the word in the British House of Commons to rail against European Union judges: 'I am glad to say, Mr Deputy Speaker, that the requirement not to be rude about judges applies only to judges in this country. It does not apply to judges in the EU [European Union], so let me be rude about them. Let me indulge in the floccinaucinihilipilification of EU judges . . .'.

Lingusitics sources trace 'floccinaucinihilipilification' back to works published as long ago as 1741, in a letter by William Shenstone, who was credited by Sir Walter Scott in 1826 as the inventor of the word. Others trace it to a 1758 Eton College Latin grammar book, the revised edition of a classic by sixteenth-century grammarian William Lily, which listed a set of words from Latin which all meant something of little value: the first four, memorably, were flocci (trivial, a wisp), nauci (a trifle, having no value), nihili (nothing), and pili (a hair, i.e., something insignificant). The story goes that some Etonians, as a jest, put all the four together to come up with a word that signified total worthlessness. But Scott misspelled it 'Floccipaucinihilipilification' (with a p as the seventh letter rather than n) and that version also persists, though the real 'f' word is the one that was the longest word in the first edition of the *Oxford English Dictionary*, and to which I seem to have given new currency in India by using it in the sentence quoted at the head of this entry.

Is the 'f' word only to be used as is? Not really: there's no reason that you can't floccinaucinihilipilify something or someone. If something is worthy of floccinaucinihilipilification, it is floccinaucical: trifling. It is in a state of floccinaucity. In more recent times the novelist Robert A. Heinlein called one of his female characters, who was always critical of things, a 'floccinaucinihilipilificatrix'. It could be a useful word for government spokesmen to dismiss the carping of critics in the Opposition: 'you can't take them seriously; they are just floccinaucinihilipilificators'. Fortunately, however, no one has fallen into the habit of uttering the 'f' word in our political discourse just yet. Maybe one day, just for the heck of it, I'll use it in parliament.

17.
Goon

noun

A BULLY OR THUG, ESPECIALLY ONE WHO
ASSAULTS OR INTIMIDATES PEOPLE

———

USAGE

The goons who assaulted students at Jawaharlal Nehru
University could not have entered and left without the
complicity of the police.

This is one word where professional English etymologists and I don't agree. I am convinced that it is a contraction of the Hindi word 'goonda', especially given the near-identical meaning.

But most Western authorities date it to an American usage in 1921, in US humorist Frederick J. Allen's piece 'The Goon and His Style' (*Harper's Monthly Magazine*, December 1921), which defines it as 'a person with a heavy touch', one who lacks 'a playful mind'. Maybe in that sense it might have descended from the sixteenth-century gony, or 'simpleton', which was applied by sailors to the albatross and similar big, clumsy birds, because a 'gooney bird' was one whose awkward way of taking off and landing made it look stupid. The word became used more widely in the US when 'goons' became characters in the 'Thimble Theater' comic strip (starring Popeye) by cartoonist E.C. Segar (1894–1938). The most famous was Alice the Goon, a slow-witted and muscular character initially depicted as a subhuman brute (but a gentle-natured one for all that).

It may well have been due to Segar's influence that the word 'goon' came to refer not just to a clumsy or awkward thickheaded person but also to a thick-muscled one, somebody of impressive physique who was hired as a 'tough guy'. In 1938, a book on American slang described a goon as a 'person of imposing physique and inferior moral and mental qualities' who usually acted as a hired 'enforcer' for a labour union, which famously led a rather rough-and-ready existence. The following year, an article in *Collier's* magazine reinforced this definition when it described members of the American Federation of Labor and Congress of Industrial Organizations (AFL-CIO) as a 'goon squad', principally for their role in beating up dissenting workers who refused to support the union's decisions. Eventually the term 'goon squad' was used to refer to any similar group of enforcers, especially in organized crime—though some on the wrong side of the law, having been on the receiving end of some punitive justice in prison, also used it to describe the police. After all, in those harsher times (when offenders were not read their rights when they were arrested), the long arm of the law often ended in a clenched fist.

However, the more commonly used sense of a bully or thug surely comes from the 'goondas' we know so well, perhaps because British POWs in German prisoner-of-war camps during the Second World War used the word 'goon' to describe their guards as unintelligent thugs. That Indian meaning of a ruffian or violent thug has long supplanted the earlier American sense of a silly, foolish, or eccentric person. Today, what most English-speakers imagine when they speak of a goon is a slow-witted, unshaven, lumbering lout hired to intimidate people. Even in the US, the word 'goon' is now widely applied to hefty thugs who accompany a mobster: 'Al Capone never appeared in public without his goon squad around him.' The British comedian Spike Milligan's *The Goon Show* (co-starring Peter Sellers) gave further currency to the word in the UK.

In India, of course, 'goon' requires no subtitles: the word, and the violent thugs themselves, are sadly ubiquitous in our country. Like its Hindi parent, goonda, a goon is not a desirable thing to be, and yet goons are widespread: bigger nasties need them, so they are available to serve bad causes for a price, often a price they extract themselves with a fist or a knife. Goons can be—and are—students, politicians, even 'leaders' in our debased political life. And they can be—and are—used to disrupt protests, beat up opponents, and intimidate decent people exercising their constitutional right to object to acts of government. They must be identified, arrested, tried and punished, if India is not to descend into a Goon(da) Raj.

18.
Hyperbole

noun

A FIGURE OF SPEECH, IN WHICH EXTREME
EXAGGERATION IS USED FOR EFFECT

———

The prime minister's promise to put Rs 15 lakh in every
Indian's bank account wasn't understood by everyone as
hyperbole, so there was a lot of disappointment when it
never happened.

Hyperbole, or an 'obvious exaggeration in rhetoric', derives from the Latin and Greek words *hyperbole*, literally meaning a 'throwing beyond', from *hyper*, meaning 'beyond', and *bole*, meaning 'a throwing or casting', thus figuratively an exaggeration or extravagance. The use of the term in its rhetorical sense goes as far back as Aristotle, where it is also known as auxesis.

Many of the best-known examples of hyperbole have become such clichés—like 'I'm so hungry I could eat a horse'—that it is always wise to avoid using them, because they have been drained of all meaning by overuse. However, hyperbole has its uses in poetry and oratory, especially of the political variety, as well as in personal conversation. The person using hyperbole does not intend to be taken literally, but rather to convey the intensity of his convictions or feelings about something—'if I'm wrong, I'll eat my hat' is a typical piece of hyperbole, often uttered by people who don't even possess a hat. The listener is also meant to understand that the statement merely conveys a feeling rather than embodying a promise.

Hyperbole is often used in casual speech as an intensifier, such as saying, 'My poor boy! His schoolbag weighs a tonne.' Hyperbole serves to make the point that the son of the speaker has an extremely heavy bag, although it obviously does not literally weigh a ton. Hyperbole can be used to convey or express humour, contempt, political views and all sorts of emotions from excitement to distress, all intending to make an effect. The American humorist Will Rogers, for instance, once combined the first three of these purposes when he said of a particular politician that, if brains were gunpowder, he wouldn't have enough to blow the wax out of his ears.

Hyperbole is a favourite tool of political speech-making, and some speakers seem given to using hyperbole much more often than necessary or even wise, as is in the case of Mr Modi's promise of Rs 15 lakhs that Amit Shah had to later explain away as a jumla. It is also used a great deal in children's writing—fairy tales and legends need the overemphasis that hyperbole provides.

Shakespeare used hyperbole quite brilliantly. Take Romeo's description of Juliet: 'The brightness of her cheek would shame those stars/As daylight doth a lamp.'

Perhaps the best use of hyperbole in contemporary writing occurs in humorous prose, because it evokes a point so well and can be funny in its own right. In *Old Times on the Mississippi*, Mark Twain wrote: 'I was helpless. I did not know what in the world to do. I was quaking from head to foot, and could have hung my hat on my eyes, they stuck out so far.' In the American folktale *Bunyan and Babe the Blue Ox*, Paul Bunyan remarks: 'Well now, one winter it was so cold that all the geese flew backward and all the fish moved south and even the snow turned blue. Late at night, it got so frigid that all spoken words froze solid afore they could be heard. People had to wait until sunup to find out what folks were talking about the night before.'

Popular American humorist and columnist Dave Barry takes hyperbole to an extreme in describing men's ability to fool themselves in *Revenge of the Pork Person*: 'A man can have a belly you could house commercial aircraft in and a grand total of eight greasy strands of hair, which he grows real long and combs across the top of his head so that he looks, when viewed from above, like an egg in the grasp of a giant spider, plus this man can have B.O. to the point where he interferes with radio transmissions, and he will still be convinced that, in terms of attractiveness, he is borderline Don Johnson.'

Obviously no part of Barry's statement and none of his analogies and metaphors can be taken literally—but the combined effect of his hyperbole means he couldn't have made his point more clearly, or humorously.

We are all accustomed to hyperbole in daily life: 'I've already told you a million times' is a typical example. Or 'I'm buried under a mountain of paperwork'. How many men, smitten by a lady whose 'mile-wide smile could melt anyone's heart', have assured women 'I'd go to the ends of the earth for you'? (Three hyperboles there—and it would surely be wrong to actually expect a lover to fulfil that commitment.) Another favourite is a host assuring unexpected guests that his wife has 'cooked enough food for an army'. And when someone tells you 'I'm so tired I could sleep for a million years', assume he or she is speaking hyperbolically, unless they are about to commit suicide.

Love, in particular, lends itself to hyperbole. But sometimes hyperbole is indeed meant to be taken seriously: 'I can't live without you' is said with great seriousness by people who genuinely mean it when they say it. Of course, they don't necessarily continue to mean it—when the time for divorce comes, they always want to go on living.

Hyperbole, as an exasperated member of the audience at one of Prime Minister Modi's speeches once said, is going to kill us all. Except that statement, too, is hyperbole . . .

19.
Impeach

verb

TO RAISE DOUBTS ABOUT, CALL INTO
QUESTION, DISCREDIT, ESPECIALLY SOMEONE'S
CREDIBILITY; TO BRING FORMAL CHARGES
AGAINST AN OFFICEHOLDER

———

USAGE

It's easy enough to impeach Trump's credibility, given the
number of lies and exaggerations he is prone to, but quite
another challenge to impeach him formally as unfit to hold
the office of President.

The word 'impeach' was very much in the news in 2020, thanks to the decision of the US House of Representatives to formally impeach the President of the United States and bring him to trial before the Senate. This has only happened twice before in US history, with the unsuccessful impeachments of Presidents Andrew Johnson in 1868 and Bill Clinton in 1998 (not counting the abortive attempt against President Richard Nixon, which he pre-empted by resigning), and the impeachment of Donald Trump has met the same fate, given his party's resounding majority in the Senate. But where does the word, with its rather fruity sound, come from?

French, it turns out. In that lovely language, *empecher* means 'to hinder, stop, impede; capture, trap, ensnare', and that's precisely what the English 'impeachment' seeks to do. In law, from the late fourteenth century, it meant broadly 'to accuse, bring charges against', but soon enough it was used to refer specifically to the king or the House of Commons, to bring a formal accusation of treason, misconduct or other high crime against a holder of a high public office.

Still, the word can also be used to refer to any person; if you are accused of misrepresenting facts, for instance, you may draw yourself to your fullest height, pierce your accuser with a furious stare, and ask, 'How dare you impeach my credibility?'

Nonetheless, it's true the word 'impeach' is most often understood as referring to holding a public official to account. And formal impeachment is usually the first step to dismissing the official from his office. But there's some confusion in most people's minds about which part of that process the word 'impeach' relates to. To make it clear, when a public official is impeached, this only means he has been charged, not convicted and removed from office. The President of the United States may be impeached by the House of Representatives, but then must be convicted by the Senate. This means the House has found reason to accuse him formally of wrongdoing; but it is the Senate that has to find him guilty.

The House of Representatives draws up articles of impeachment that itemize the charges and their factual basis. The articles of impeachment, if approved by a simple majority of the members of the House, are then submitted to the Senate, thereby impeaching the President. The Senate then holds a trial, at the conclusion of which each member votes for or against conviction on each article of impeachment.

Two-thirds of the Senate members present must vote in favour of conviction. Once convicted, the President is automatically removed from office. This has never happened in the US, though it has succeeded in a few Latin American countries, when maverick presidents ran afoul of legislatures which were in the hands of established political parties.

Most people wrongly assume that to 'impeach' a President or other high official is to assume his guilt and even dismiss him. Though in some countries the individual is provisionally removed, this is rare, and impeachment is normally not the punishment; it merely precedes the trial.

Impeaching someone sets in motion a legal process that may or may not conclude wrongdoing has taken place and result in a conviction. Since that decision is made, in the US as in India, by elected legislators rather than qualified judges, it is always a political rather than a judicial verdict. That is why it may not make much sense to resort to it unless you are sure beforehand that you have the numbers to prevail.

President Andrew Johnson was acquitted in 1868, by one vote, of violating the previous year's Tenure of Office Act. President Bill Clinton was acquitted in 1998, by a much larger margin, of charges of perjury and obstructing justice in relation to the Monica Lewinsky sex scandal.

President Richard Nixon, however, resigned to avoid inevitable impeachment for the Watergate scandal, and was granted an unconditional pardon by his successor, Gerald Ford. The chances of President Trump finding a two-thirds majority against him in a Republican-dominated Senate were widely seen as close to zero, and indeed he survived in a largely party-line vote.

Students of Indian history may have noticed that the British have not been impeaching anybody since the famous impeachment of

Warren Hastings for his misconduct in India as the East India Company's Governor-General. At the time, impeachment was the trial of an individual by the House of Lords at the request of the House of Commons and was commonly used as a way to fight out battles between Crown and Parliament.

The British Parliament gave up the practice officially in 1806, partly because several high-profile trials, including that of Hastings (which dragged on for seven years but ended in acquittal), were considered to have brought it into disrepute. The Indian Parliament can also impeach high officials, including the President and judges; it has never done so, its attempts to impeach a judge having prompted that individual's premature resignation.

Because impeachment and conviction of officials involve the overturning of the normal constitutional procedures by which individuals achieve high office (election, ratification, or appointment) and because it generally requires a two-thirds or similar majority, impeachment is usually reserved for those considered to have committed serious abuses of their public position.

Impeachment exists under constitutional law in many countries around the world, including, aside from the United States and India, Brazil, France, Ireland, the Philippines, Russia and South Korea (which recently successfully impeached and jailed a President for corruption).

screech

crash

20.
Jaywalking

noun

TO CROSS THE STREET AGAINST THE TRAFFIC
REGULATIONS, ILLEGALLY, AGAINST A RED
LIGHT OR IN THE MIDDLE OF THE STREET

USAGE

The Indian tourist was surprised to be arrested
for jaywalking, when that was how he had been
brought up to cross the road.

Whatever may be our political differences, all Indians have one thing in common: jaywalking. We are all inveterate jaywalkers. Traffic lights for pedestrians exist, but are universally ignored. Oddly enough, though, we don't use the word for this practice— perhaps precisely because it is so common we didn't feel we needed a special word for it.

The word jaywalker can be traced back to 1912, when it emerged in American English, derived, probably, from the bird of that name, the common blue jay. (The theory that the term jaywalking is derived from the shape of the letter 'J' to describe the erratic path a jaywalker might travel when crossing a road, has been discredited, since jaywalkers can also walk straight, but do so when or where they are not supposed to.)

'Jay' was an insulting term in colloquial English for a foolish chattering person back in the 1500s, and in the US was used to refer to a stupid, gullible, ignorant, or provincial person, a rustic, or simpleton. It seems city-dwellers assumed that those who crossed the roads when they weren't supposed to had to be country bumpkins who didn't know any better, hence 'jaywalkers'. The connotation of 'jay' was that it applied to a naïve individual, a 'hick', who didn't know the ropes of modern, civilized, urban living.

In the early years of automobiles there was also the expression 'jay drivers' for those who wandered about all over the road, causing confusion among other drivers and creating accidents. Strict rules, strictly enforced, about which side of the road one could drive on, put an end to jay driving. However, jaywalking has continued.

In the second decade of the twentieth century the new term 'jaywalkers' emerged, as city councils in the US began to pass ordinances to stop pedestrians crossing the street anywhere they wanted to. Apparently, the rapid increase in motorized vehicular traffic made the adoption of such regulations necessary. The public was strongly in favour. One newspaper report from 1911 defines a jaywalker as 'an alleged human being who crosses the street at other points than the regular crossings'. Another writes: 'Jay Walker is aptly named—he remains unconvinced that traffic lights apply to pedestrians.' A 1937 *New York Times* article sneers, 'In many streets like Oxford Street, for instance, the jaywalker wanders complacently in the very middle of the roadway as if it was a country lane.'

Automobile companies popularly used this term in various anti-pedestrian advertising campaigns. For instance, John Hertz, president of Yellow Cab and the future founder of the country's leading car rental firm, declared, 'We fear the "jay walker" worse than the anarchist, and Chicago is his native home.' The campaigns worked: in the US, the automobile companies won the right to use of roads and to restrict pedestrian access to them. Jaywalking is a crime pretty much everywhere in the US, attracting severe fines.

There are laws against jaywalking in the US, Singapore, Poland, Serbia, Iran, Australia and New Zealand. However, in many countries in the world besides India, it's perfectly legal to cross any road anywhere you like, whenever you judge it to be safe to do so. Ironically, many advocates argue that jaywalkers tend to be more careful when crossing the road than those who are crossing in officially designated crosswalks.

Still, even in the US, jaywalking is seen as referring to a relatively insignificant crime. As in, 'compared to the man in the Oval Office, his principal rival has done little wrong, nothing more serious than jaywalking'.

However minor it may be, don't try jaywalking in the US or Singapore. Ignorance of the law, the police in those countries insist, is no excuse. I know: I've been caught there.

21.
Juggernaut

noun

AN UNSTOPPABLE, RELENTLESS MOVING FORCE
THAT DESTROYS ANYTHING IN ITS PATH

USAGE

When the German stormtroopers marched into Poland, the
hapless Poles proved unable to resist the Nazi juggernaut.

Though the word looks vaguely Germanic, 'juggernaut' is actually a mangling of 'Jagannath', the name of the deity carried in devotional procession in Odisha four times a year in elaborate yatras on land and water, of which the most famous is the rath yatra, or chariot procession in the Hindu month of Ashadha. This is when the idol is wheeled to the Puri temple in an enormous chariot as devotees line the streets in a frenzy, hailing the Lord with chants and prayers and craning their necks for a glimpse of the deity seated in the chariot, followed by lesser chariots bearing statues of his brother Balarama and sister Subhadra. 'Juggernaut', therefore, derives from Sanskrit, not German: its roots are the Sanskrit *jagat*, or 'world', and *natha*, meaning 'lord, master'. The Lord of the World is, of course, Lord Krishna.

Orientalism began early, alas: four centuries *before* the British conquest of India began, falsely distorted tales about India were propagated in the fourteenth-century travelogue of Sir John Mandeville, who described the festival in his *Travels of Sir John Mandeville* and depicted Hindus throwing themselves under the wheels of the enormous Jagannath chariots as a religious sacrifice and being crushed to death.

Sir John may have been echoing the first European description of the rath yatra festival from a thirteenth-century account by the Franciscan monk and missionary Odoric of Pordenone. But Hinduism in fact has no concept of such human sacrifice; if either Odoric or the eponymous Sir John really saw a Hindu killed under the wheels of a chariot, it can only be because a poor devotee stumbled or was pushed by the throng and fell accidentally upon the path in the tumult, and the enormous chariot could not easily stop or turn on the narrow road.

Still, the tale, the false image of the faith it portrayed, and the unfortunate associations of the word persisted. By the eighteenth century, 'juggernaut' was in common use as a synonym for an irresistible and destructive force that demands total devotion or unforgiving sacrifice—the sense in which it pops up in the novels of Charlotte Bronte and Charles Dickens, and even Robert Louis Stevenson, who applied it to Dr Jekyll's foil, Mr Hyde.

Today, its usage is largely metaphorical: a juggernaut is something remorseless and implacable, a merciless, destructive and unstoppable force that demands blind devotion or absolute sacrifice. Its synonyms are words like 'steamroller' and 'battering ram'. It is still extensively used, in references to 'the Chinese economic juggernaut' or 'the Obama electoral juggernaut'. 'Who can stop the Federer juggernaut at Wimbledon?' mused a sportswriter. It is said that 'Hollywood film producers are helpless in the face of the box office juggernaut'. So juggernaut, in contemporary usage, is always associated with an overwhelming force, neutral or more often negative, that cannot be stopped and you can do nothing about. Marvel Comics even has a supervillain named Juggernaut in its *X-Men* comics. To non-Indian users of the English language, juggernaut always represents power, violence, death and relentlessness.

These negative associations were explicitly reinforced in the colonial era by a nineteenth-century Anglican missionary, Rev. Claudius Buchanan, who popularized the term in a series of letters and articles in the British and American press. His gory descriptions of human sacrifice and comparisons of juggernaut to the Biblical Moloch were intended to justify the need for spreading Christianity in India: Juggernaut, to him, was a symbol of Hinduism's violence, bloodshed, death and 'idolatry'.

In its present form, therefore, the word is devoid of any real association with Lord Jagannath: 'Juggernaut' in today's usage is quite simply a product of the British and American imagination, and no reflection of Indian reality. It was only Mark Twain, in his *Autobiography*, who described Juggernaut as the kindest of gods; and indeed the millions of worshippers in Puri will tell you that Lord Jagannath is a figure of reverence, not of fear. But alas, by then the damage had been done, and 'juggernaut' had passed (yes, unstoppably!) into the English language.

22.
Kakistocracy

noun

A FORM OF GOVERNMENT IN WHICH THE
LEAST QUALIFIED OR MOST UNPRINCIPLED
INDIVIDUALS ARE IN POWER

———

USAGE

Sometimes, in recent years, it has seemed that
the world's largest democracy has in many ways
degenerated into a kakistocracy.

Derived from the ancient Greek—the speakers of which were pioneers of democratic practice and knew a thing or two about good governance, or the lack thereof—a 'kakistocracy' is a government by the worst elements in society. The word comes from the Greek *kakistos*, which is the superlative form of the word *kakos*, meaning 'bad'; *kakistos* means as bad as it can possibly get.

There's even a suggestion that *kakos* comes from the ancient proto-Indo-European root '*kakka*', meaning what you produce when you defecate (a sense in which it is still used in many Indian languages, at least colloquially). Related words in ancient Greek were *kakonomia*, meaning 'a bad system of laws and government', which in turn gave the ancient Greeks the descriptive expression *kakonomos*, applicable to a place 'with bad laws, ill-governed'.

Kakistocracy, a word in use since the seventeenth century and made popular by Thomas Love Peacock in the early nineteenth, was coined as the opposite of aristocracy, which is made up of Greek *aristos*, or 'best', and *cratia*, 'rule'. Of course, there was an upper-class snootiness about the rise of democracy behind the use of the term: whereas rule by aristocrats was supposed to involve the dominance of the best elements of society, democracy, it was suggested, often unleashed the worst. In our more egalitarian times, aristocracy no longer carries an association of approbation, though its opposite is, of course, even worse, and given its etymological roots, kakistocracy could never be considered a positive term.

The US has long been fertile territory for the use of the word kakistocracy. The American poet James Russell Lowell wrote in a letter in 1876: 'Is ours a "government of the people, by the people, for the people", or a Kakistocracy, rather for the benefit of knaves at the cost of fools?' In 1944, *Time* magazine hoped that the introduction of voting machines would challenge 'the very vitals of the kakistocracy' running the corrupt regime of the New Jersey Democratic party boss, Frank Hague.

American columnists have lately resurrected the word 'kakistocracy' to discuss the rule of President Donald J. Trump, whose manner, policies and tweets seem to evoke fear and loathing in equal measure amongst large numbers of the US chatterati. Populism is often condemned as resulting in kakistocracy, since populists are perceived as coming to power by appealing to the worst instincts, prejudices and ignorant biases of their voters. When a former CIA director, John Brennan, described Donald Trump on Twitter as running a 'kakistocracy', it reportedly sparked a 13,700 per cent increase in people looking up the word on the online version of the Merriam-Webster dictionary.

Of course, America is not the only laboratory of kakistocracy, which can be found wherever expertise, education and ethics are abandoned in favour of short-term popularity, crude appeals to the worst instincts of a people and low standards of governance. The English writer John Martineau, in his 1869 publication *Letters from Australia*, lamenting the poor quality of the civil service Down Under, the self-serving politicians and the coarse political debate, wondered whether Australia would become a kakistocracy.

It hasn't, arguably. But in recent years, many of us have been wondering whether our India has. The word kakistocracy has not been used much in India, despite us seeing in high places people who declare they want to replace Mahatma Gandhi's statues with his assassin Nathuram Godse's, destroy or exile the entire Muslim community, or send critics to Pakistan, preferably attached to the wrong end of a bomb. Not to mention those in our ruling circles who believe in the virus-curing properties of cow urine, advocate standing in the sun for fifteen minutes to avoid contagion, and believe our Vedic ancestors invented jet engines, interstellar travel and GPS. Maybe it's time we too dusted off the term.

23.
Kerfuffle

noun

A DISORDERLY OUTBURST, TUMULT, ROW,
RUCKUS OR DISTURBANCE; A DISORDER,
FLURRY, OR AGITATION; A FUSS

———

USAGE

In view of the kerfuffle around my tweet wrongly
attributing to the US a picture of Nehruji in the USSR,
I thought it best to tweet some pictures that really
showed him in the US.

Kerfuffle turns out to quite commonly used in Scots, the language of Scotland, and is an intensive form of the Scots word '*fuffle*,' meaning 'to disturb'. The modern word comes from the Scottish '*curfuffle*' by way of earlier similar expressions that were spelt variously as *curfuffle*, *carfuffle*, *cafuffle*, *cafoufle*, even *gefuffle*. This suggests that the word was mainly used orally and that it was usually transmitted through conversational usage rather than written language—such expressions in popular speech often were spelled differently when people bothered to write them down, which is why it took till the 1960s for the standard spelling of kerfuffle to be established.

The word 'kerfuffle' is much more commonly used in Britain and the Commonwealth than in the US. It is said that when the younger President Bush used 'kerfuffle' in 2006 during an appearance in Ohio, he created a minor kerfuffle himself, because television channels broadcasting his remarks live had to interrupt their shows to explain the word to Middle America. (This is not entirely surprising, after all, since Bush 43, as he was known, and who had, after all, coined the Bushism 'misunderestimated', was not exactly famous for using the language correctly.)

There's something about the sound of the word kerfuffle that also lends itself to slightly dismissive usage—a kerfuffle is not just a fuss but a fuss that should not be taken too seriously. I used it, for instance, to refer to the huge fuss made about my misattributed photo on Twitter, because this kerfuffle was a distraction from the real debate that we should have been having, which was whether the public turnout for an Indian prime minister in a foreign country was in any way unprecedented. What Brits might call 'a storm in a teacup' can be called a kerfuffle. But a major clash, serious disagreement or monumental fiasco should not be termed a mere kerfuffle, since that would diminish it in the telling.

So save 'kerfuffle' for a trivial row, or an unjustified or exaggerated ruckus. There are plenty of those in social media anyway, all serving as weapons of mass distraction, to take the public's minds off the real problems we should all be dealing with. Maybe my saying that will cause another kerfuffle!

24.
Lethologica

noun

THE AFFLICTION OF NOT REMEMBERING
THE RIGHT WORD FOR THE THOUGHT
YOU ARE TRYING TO EXPRESS

———

USAGE

He was usually never at a loss for words, but right in
the middle of an important interview, he suffered
a crippling bout of lethologica.

Lethologica happens to everyone—yes, even me! How many of us have gone through that awful feeling when you think of something you know well and wish to convey precisely to the person you are speaking to, but the word for it escapes you? Lethologica is not the same as simply mixing up similar-sounding words, as when people say 'reticence' when they mean 'reluctance', a common error. It's when the word you want is trembling at the tip of your tongue but your mind is simply unable to dredge it up from all the many times you have heard or used it before. This too is pretty common: according to the American Psychiatry Association, nine out of ten people will suffer some form of lethologica during their lifetimes.

Lethologica is derived from the Ancient Greek word *lethe*, 'forgetfulness', and another Greek term, *logikos*, which means 'of or relating to thought or reason' (some also relate it to *logos*, or 'word'). There's a great story about the first part of the word lethologica. The Lethe, known as the River of Oblivion, was one of the rivers that flowed through the realm of Hades, the hellish underworld to which, in Greek mythology, you were banished in death. In these tales, the dead were forced to drink from the waters of the Lethe river in order to forget their past lives on earth.

The affliction of an inability to remember the proper word was first identified as a disorder by the famous Swiss psychiatrist Carl Jung in a 1913 study. But it's really far too common a problem to be elevated to the medical textbooks. It's also not incurable—though usually you struggle to remember the right word, and the harder you try, the more elusive it gets. (In the worst cases, that can lead to *loganamnosis*—when the sufferer from lethogica is so obsessed with trying to remember the word that she couldn't recall to the point where she's unable to pay attention to the rest of the conversation.)

With so much to watch on television these days, especially a wide choice of entertainment on streaming platforms like Netflix and Amazon, many also suffer from lethonomia, the inability to recall the right name. It's a harmless enough failing—unless, of course, you happen to be a politician, in which case forgetting the name of a party worker or a constituent is tantamount to ensuring the loss of his or her support.

I suspect most of my readers will have had an experience of lethologica. You're talking about someone or something, a situation or a problem, and you are just about to use the word to describe it—and then suddenly you hit a blank. But just when you have parted from the friend you were speaking to—that's when the words pops up, miraculously and frustratingly. Or worse, just when you are falling asleep, the mind goes, 'Eureka! That's it! The word for not remembering the right word—it's lethologica!'

25.
Luddite

noun

ONE WHO STRONGLY OPPOSES (OR AT LEAST
AVOIDS) THE USE OF NEW TECHNOLOGY

———

USAGE

My aunt is a Luddite; she still refuses to have a mobile
phone and insists on retaining her old rotary-dial
telephone from the 1960s.

The term comes from the Luddites, a group of angry and radical textile workers in England who, during a region-wide rebellion from 1811 to 1816, destroyed machinery that was causing them to lose their jobs. It is said they were inspired (but apparently not led) by Ned Ludd of Nottingham, who had acquired some notoriety by destroying, in a fit of rage (or insanity, depending on who was telling the story), a knitting frame in 1779. Luddites argued that the new machines were anti-humanity, since they would displace people, while the many years workers spent learning the skills of their craft would be wasted once automated textile equipment took over their roles. The Luddite insurrection did not go unpunished; factory and mill-owners started shooting protesters, armed soldiers were called in and in response to their spree of destruction, the British Parliament passed the Frame-Breaking Act which made the destruction of knitting frames punishable by death.

The Luddite movement may have died out soon enough, but the name clung to those who opposed many forms of modern technology over the following two centuries. In India, the communist cadres who smashed computers when they were first introduced into LIC offices and public sector banks in the 1980s did so for exactly the same reasons as their forebears in Nottingham in 1811—they feared the new machines would replace them in their jobs and make their mathematical and computational skills irrelevant. They were Indian Luddites. Today the word is also used more irreverently to refer to anyone resistant to technology; housewives who won't trust microwave ovens, parents who don't WhatsApp, middle-aged resisters of smartphones and the like can all be described as Luddites.

But there are still some serious Luddites around, who don't agree with the way modern technology is transforming our lives. In April 1996, the Second Luddite Congress met in Barnesville, Ohio, and issued a manifesto proclaiming the birth of Neo-Luddism as 'a leaderless movement of passive resistance to consumerism and the increasingly bizarre and frightening technologies of the Computer Age'. As with all leaderless movements, however, the Neo-Luddites seem to have faded away without a whimper; Google, another technology they no doubt oppose, records no mention of a Third Luddite Congress.

26.
Lunacy

noun

THE CONDITION OF BEING A LUNATIC;
MENTAL UNSOUNDNESS

———

USAGE

This was an act of sheer lunacy on his part;
what he said and did made no sense and can
only be blamed on a bout of insanity.

The moon, in most Indian languages, is a romantic object, associated with love and dreams, and often applied to rare and exceptional individuals—'chaundvi ka chand', 'Eid ka chand' tend to be used in a complimentary sense, and popular names like Chand, Chander/Chandran, and Shashi/Shashikant/Shashank, all derive from that celestial orb.

But in mediaeval English, lunacy referred to intermittent periods of insanity, believed to be triggered by the moon's cycle, rather as animals were said to bay madly on full moon nights. This came in turn from the Old French *lunatique*, meaning insane, which was derived from the late Latin *lunaticus*, or 'moonstruck' (*luna* is the Latin for 'moon'). In those days people thought that mental illness, neurological disorders and even epilepsy were related to the waxing and waning of the moon. The Greek philosopher Aristotle and the Roman historian Pliny the Elder suggested that the brain was the 'moistest' organ in the body and so most vulnerable to the pernicious influences of the moon, which triggers the tides. In the Middle Ages, many believed that some humans were transformed into werewolves or vampires during a full moon.

Perhaps this association was because a full moon brought light into the night, thereby confusing animals—and some human beings—with brightness when they were accustomed to darkness, and thus throwing their minds into confusion. As Shakespeare says in *Othello*:

> '*It is the very error of the moon.*
> *She comes more near the earth than she was wont.*
> *And makes men mad.*'

The idea that lunacy involves acts of madness or folly persisted, even though the correlation between sanity and the phases of the moon stopped being taken seriously in modern times. Typically, some American scholars decided to research the subject: two psychologists and an astronomer did a detailed meta-analysis of the moon's effects on human behaviour, and their 1985 review of thirty-seven studies entitled 'Much Ado about the Full

Moon', in the major peer-reviewed journal, *Psychological Bulletin*, concluded that no effect could be proven and further research was unnecessary. The moon might move the tides, and it even influences the mating cycles of corals and glow-worms, but not, despite all the myths, of humans—not even adolescents.

The term 'lunacy' persisted through the last century, though. Lawyers used it to refer to unsoundness of mind that might make a person incapable of managing their affairs or concluding civil transactions. Indeed, the word 'lunatic' appeared in British laws—and therefore in Indian ones—well into the twentieth century, and it was only in 2012 that the US House of Representatives passed legislation (approved earlier by the Senate) removing the word 'lunatic' from all federal laws in the US. Today, 'of unsound mind' or the Latin expression *non compos mentis* is preferred by the courts to 'lunatic'.

Today it is widely accepted that 'lunatic' is an obsolete term that is not used any more to refer to persons suffering from mental illness. 'Lunacy' survives, but only in metaphorical and often jocular usage; to use it literally as a synonym for 'insanity' would, at the very least, be considered impolite. It's totally normal to enjoy looking at the moon! (Of course, Shashi would say that . . .)

27.
Lynch

verb

INFLICT SEVERE, AND OFTEN FATAL,
BODILY PUNISHMENT ON SOMEONE,
WITHOUT LEGAL SANCTION

———

USAGE

The mob lynched a man accused of slaughtering
a cow, even while he protested that the meat he
was carrying was that of a buffalo.

The word 'lynch', like 'boycott' and 'macadam', comes from the name of a person. In this case, there are two possible claimants for this eponymous distinction.

The expression derives from the American Lynch law of 1811, covering punishment without trial, named after either William Lynch (1742–1820) of Virginia, who in about 1780 led a vigilance committee to keep order in his home town of Pittsylvania during the American Revolution, or Charles Lynch (1736–96), a pro-revolutionary Virginia magistrate who fined and imprisoned British loyalists in his district without trial at about the same time, and got a law passed by the American government exonerating him for his actions.

A nineteenth-century dictionary, the *Century Dictionary*, published in 1895, defines lynching as 'lawless concert or action among a number of members of the community, to supply the want of criminal justice or to anticipate its delays, or to inflict a penalty demanded by public opinion, though in defiance of the laws'.

Lynching involves what is often called 'mob justice', since it is always conducted by a mob, and always in the name of executing an act of 'justice' that the authorities are deemed to be too soft, too cautious (or too hamstrung by due process) to execute themselves.

Lynching dispenses summary justice, often unjustly, and without the authority of the law, in retribution for a crime or public offence. In America this usually included flogging and 'tarring-and-feathering', where the targeted person was doused in liquid tar and feathers were stuck all over his person, so when the tar dried he was reduced to a figure of ridicule and paraded through the town to be hissed at for his sins. At first this kind of action targeted people suspected of crimes in the frontier regions of the Wild West, though soon enough the target list was broadened to include slave owners lynching abolitionists and blacks trying to escape slavery, who were often hanged in public for their efforts (racial lynching).

After the Civil War and the abolition of slavery, lynching became associated with 'showing uppity blacks their place', and was frequently resorted to by white supremacists against blacks accused of asserting their rights or showing undue familiarity to white women. By the late nineteenth century, a 'lynching' thus came to mean 'extra-legal execution by hanging' (especially in retaliation for alleged sexual assaults of white women).

Lynching is now universally understood to refer to the premeditated extrajudicial killing of people by a mob or group of people, usually from a different religious or ethnic community, and involves public executions by a mob in order to punish an alleged transgressor, or to intimidate the group to which the victim belongs. It is usually conducted in public in order to ensure maximum intimidatory effect. It is estimated that nearly 3500 African Americans and 1300 whites were lynched in the United States between 1882 and 1968.

Indian lynchings have most often aimed, in recent years, at Muslims and Dalits; well-known examples include the Khairlanji lynching of a Dalit family in 2006, and the lynching of Muslims accused of cow slaughter in UP, Rajasthan, Jharkhand and other states in the Hindi belt. In Dimapur, Nagaland, a mob broke into a jail and lynched an accused rapist in 2015 while he was awaiting trial. There were also several 'WhatsApp lynchings' in 2017 following the spread of fake news on social media about child abduction and organ harvesting;

the victims even included a government official sent to a village in West Bengal to reassure people the rumours were untrue.

In other countries with high crime rates, notably in Latin America, victims are often criminals who the mobs feel would otherwise escape justice; lynchings here are another form of 'vigilante justice' reflecting lack of faith in law enforcement or judicial institutions.

Some argue that a decline in economic conditions is enough to spur lynch mobs, though others argue that communal hatred is usually enough.

While lynching is always illegal, perpetrators often escape justice, partly because of public support for their actions and partly because it is difficult to pin criminal responsibility on a mob. Attempts in parliament by MPs, including myself, to initiate private member's bills to provide for an anti-lynching law have been unable to make headway so far.

Meanwhile, as Delhi knows too well, mob violence goes on—and, in the process, it is our democracy that is lynched.

28.
Muliebrity

noun

WOMANHOOD, WOMANLINESS, FEMININITY, THE CONDITION OF BEING A WOMAN OR BEHAVING IN WAYS CONSIDERED TYPICAL OF A WOMAN. THE ANTONYM OF VIRILITY

USAGE

His mother embodied all the qualities of gentle nurturing, devotion, uncritical affection and fine cooking that he associated with muliebrity.

The word 'muliebrity' goes back to the late sixteenth century, and is derived from the Latin *muliebritas* or womanhood, in turn a derivative of *mulier* or woman. There is an adjective form, *muliebral*, 'of or pertaining to a woman'. Neither word is widely used any more, but as a valid word in the language, muliebrity can be applied to all women, and to all men who behave like women.

This is where we start venturing into sexist territory, however. What does 'behaving like women' mean?

The word's root *mulier*, 'a woman', is traditionally said to derive from *mollis*, meaning soft or weak. In old legal language, mulier was used as a noun to refer to 'a woman; a wife', and as an adjective, to mean 'born in wedlock'. (A mulier offspring, or just a mulier, was a legitimate child according to ecclesiastical law.) For a while the word muliebrious was used as a synonym for 'effeminate'—'that muliebrious fashion designer', for instance. A paid legion of trolls accuse me daily on social media of mulierosity, without ever using the word (which means an excessive fondness for women, but they don't know that and so have to rely on cruder vulgarisms to convey the same charge).

The problem with the word muliebrity is that it brings a lot of baggage with it, consisting mainly of rather sexist ideas about what is womanly. Muliebrity embraces notions of soft, gentle, 'feminine' characteristics that many women bridle at—and that may be far from the lived experience of those men who have grown up with, or are married to, strong women. When the word is applied to men, it implies effeminate ways, heavy make-up, outlandish clothing and the like. The very notion of muliebrity is based on old-fashioned concepts of feminine behaviour that the world has largely outgrown, outside a few *khap panchayats* in our Bimaru states.

But that may be precisely why the word muliebrity might have a longer run in Indian English than in the West, since we, as a society, are slower to let go of the gender stereotypes and expectations of womanhood that come with it. Bollywood films are still full of muliebrious or over-feminine women, though exceptions have broken through in recent years. And the Sati-Savitri ideal of womanhood is the classic epitome of muliebrity, reinforced in countless cultural tropes over the years.

A friend I tried the word out on—'what do you think muliebrity means?'—understandably thought it meant stubbornness, because of the association of that quality with mules. He would no doubt have been surprised to learn that Vanderbilt University in the US offers the Muliebrity Prize to honour students who 'demonstrate leadership in activities that contribute to the achievements, interests and goals of women and girls, or that promote equity'. Muliebrity, of course, has nothing to do with mules. But certainly some stubbornness would come in handy when women fight for their rights in a patriarchal system. I remain of the view that the Women's Reservation Bill would guarantee the entry of the irresistible muliebral force that has been largely missing from our male-dominated parliament.

Interestingly, there is a specifically Indian example of the use of the word.

'Muliebrity' is the title of a poem by Sujata Bhatt that describes the sight of a young girl in our country who spends her days picking up cow dung, and the inherent 'glistening' power she has as a female.

The poem expands our ideas of what it means to be a woman.

Ultimately, of course, your muliebrity is best expressed not by dressing in a certain manner, walking in a feminine way or making your speech and conduct conform to the expectations of men, but by being your own true self as a woman and as a human being.

29.
Namaste

noun

GESTURE OF GREETING OR SALUTATION MADE
BY BRINGING THE PALMS TOGETHER AND
BOWING, COMMONLY PRACTISED IN INDIA

———

USAGE

As I offered my guru a respectful namaste, I was conscious
that my gesture was telling him, 'the sacred in me
recognizes the sacred in you'.

As health authorities around the world advise people to avoid shaking hands (and even to eschew Prime Minister Modi's preferred bear hug) to minimize the risk of being infected by the highly contagious coronavirus, the Indian *namaskaram*, more commonly known as namaste, offers the preferred alternative.

This common desi salutation is now quite being considered the safest and most 'virus-proof' way to greet people. While various other gestures—from using shod feet instead of bare hands to touch the other person, to elbow bumps and knuckle thumps—have also been tried, many world leaders have shown a distinct preference for India's traditional folded-hands greeting.

'Namaste goes global', understandably chuffed Indian headlines screamed as world leaders including US President Donald Trump, French President Emmanuel Macron and Britain's Prince Charles adopted it on widely televised occasions during the coronavirus pandemic. With palms pressed together and a little bow, Macron received Spain's King Felipe and Queen Letizia at the Elysee Palace in Paris even as his ambassador to New Delhi, Emmanuel Lenain, tweeted, 'President Macron has decided to greet all his counterparts with a namaste, a graceful gesture that he has retained from his India visit in 2018.'

When Trump greeted Irish Prime Minister Leo Varadkar at the White House recently, it was with a namaste. While that should have been easy for the half-Indian Irish PM, Varadkar said, 'It almost feels impersonal. It feels like you're being rude.'

This is no small matter, since the customary handshake is what provides world leaders the usual photo opportunity that is publicized around the world to mark their meetings. Trump admitted that it was 'sort of a weird feeling' to forego the handshake. Britain's Prince Charles, son and heir of the Queen, nearly forgot during a recent meeting with the lord lieutenant of Greater London, offering a handshake before quickly remembering to switch to a namaste. 'It's just so hard to remember not to [shake hands],' he reportedly muttered.

But Israeli Prime Minister Benjamin Netanyahu had no hesitation in recommending the Indian namaste to his fellow citizens with a televisual demonstration at a press conference. He said it was one of the simplest ways to prevent the virus from spreading.

India is hardly alone in having devised a greeting that does not involve the vigorous pumping of hands. The Japanese have the custom of *ojigi*—bowing to each other, with the depth of the bowing conveying the degree of respect in a hierarchical society. Tibetans stick out their tongues in greeting, while Eskimos rub noses. In Oman, Qatar and Yemen people touch their noses in a salaam to others. Some Arabs hug each other, the greeter's head crossing one shoulder after another. The Europeans, of course, famously kiss each other on the cheeks, though usually they are kissing air alongside the other's cheek. But if you want to greet someone while avoiding close contact or even proximity with the other in order to prevent coronavirus, nothing beats the namaste.

The ancient Indian greeting conveys respect while maintaining a distance. As I pointed out in a tweet, behind every major ancient Indian tradition, there is science. I should have added spirituality, since 'namaste' is not just a gesture of greeting. It is one of the six forms of *pranama* in Hinduism and conveys that the person one is greeting, even a stranger, shares a common Atman with you, so that 'the divine in me bows [in greeting and recognition] to the divine in you'.

The term 'namaste' (*Namas*+*te*) is derived from Sanskrit and is a combination of the word *namas* and the second person dative pronoun, *te*, in what linguists call its enclitic form. *Namaḥ* means 'bow' or 'obeisance' and *te* means 'to you'. It is a specific way of bowing to the other, thus showing respect, and at the same time (unlike, say, prostrating yourself and touching the other's feet), conveys that one is equal to the other as shards of the same soul. In saying namaste, we signal that the divinity within oneself is the 'same' in the other, since it is all-pervasive. The namaste sees and adores the divine in every person, and is therefore an act of both humility and spiritual bonding.

What could be more appropriate today than this message of universal brotherhood, from the very culture that proclaimed '*Vasudhaiva kutumbakam*' (the whole world is a family)? As COVID-19 assails us all, we're all in this together. No one's passport makes him exempt from the risk of contagion. We share the same divinity, the same soul, and the same vulnerability. Namaste to you, dear reader—wherever you are.

30.
Nerd

noun

A WONK OR GEEK, OBSESSIVELY IMMERSED IN AND KNOWLEDGEABLE ABOUT A NARROW SUBJECT, BUT LACKING SOCIAL SKILLS

———

USAGE

That nerd is not someone I enjoy talking to, but he knows more about computers than you or I do, so I need him.

The word 'nerd' became a fixture of US student slang in the 1960s. The *Oxford English Dictionary* says 'Origin uncertain and disputed'. But American sources are pretty sure: they date it to 1951, when it first showed up in US student slang, perhaps changing an earlier slang word 'nert', which itself altered the expression 'nut' to refer to a stupid or crazy person.

Where did kids dream up the word 'nerd'? It seems to have come from Nerd, a fictional animal in the children's story *If I Ran the Zoo* (1950) by the madly popular children's writer Dr Seuss (Theodor Seuss Geisel). It occurs in his verse: *'And then, just to show them, I'll sail to Katroo, And bring back an It-Kutch, a Preep and a Proo, A Nerkle, a Nerd and a Seersucker too!'*

Dr Seuss, who did his own illustrations, depicts the Nerd as a tiny, unkempt, vaguely human-looking creature with a large head and a strange expression. The word promptly started to be applied on American college campuses. A year later, *Newsweek* reported on the word's popularity on campus: '. . . someone who once would be called a drip or a square is now, regrettably, a nerd.' Some suggest that collegians actually spelt 'drunk' backwards to describe such an over-sober character who studiously didn't drink or socialize ('knurd'). Whichever version is accurate, 'nerds' are now here to stay.

The primary characteristics of nerds are that they know a lot about some subject, usually a highly technical one that's little known and often non-mainstream, prefer studying over partying, and are worthless company, though highly useful when you need their expertise. They have no social graces, can be introverted, boring and dress unattractively.

But there's a difference between a geek and a nerd, though both are knowledgeable and intelligent. A geek can talk to people, sometimes brilliantly, and rise in the world (*Time* magazine ran a headline in 1995 declaring 'The Geek Shall Inherit the Earth'). A nerd, on the other hand, obsesses about one thing but is hopeless at everything else. Geeks are always techies, but knowledge of technology is not essential to be a nerd; a nerd is just extremely focused on his area of expertise, brainy but socially inept. Nerds are geeks without social skills. But you can be a 'movie geek' or a 'music geek', which makes you desirable company on the social scene for those interested in movies or music. (I'm a bit of a 'cricket geek' myself.)

But the word 'nerd' is still more complimentary than two other examples of American slang with negative connotations, 'dork' and 'dweeb'. No one would call themselves a 'computer dork', but a 'computer nerd' is not such a bad thing to be. In fact, experts on usage say that 'nerd' is popularly used to describe academic expertise in a subject, as in 'language nerd', or 'chemistry nerd', and being a nerd can be a badge of pride. It's a word that implies that you possess a depth of knowledge in the particular area you're obsessed about. And in the era of Artificial Intelligence, it's not uncool to possess the real thing.

Still, labelling a kid a nerd at school, merely because they show their intellect, can be harmful. Some bright kids deliberately suppress their intellectual leanings for fear of being branded as nerds. Aside from seeking social acceptability, it's a measure of self-protection; in many schools, 'nerds' are the target of bullying because of their social ineptitude and lack of popularity (and a certain amount of envy on the part of the popular jocks, whom the nerds outshine in class). Nerds, often, are too narrowly fixated on their subject of interest to have the time for the activities required to be popular.

It doesn't help that nerds are also assumed to have an unattractive physical appearance, caricatured as being physically unfit, skinny or fat from lack of exercise, having buck teeth and acne, and wearing very large glasses, braces and pants pulled up high at the waist. The Unicode emoticon for a 'Nerd Face' released in 2015 reflects some of those stereotypes:

In the United States, racism has crept into popular understandings of nerdiness: a 2010 study published in the *Journal of International and Intercultural Communication* says that Asian Americans are perceived as most likely to be nerds. Those Indians who have watched Kunal Nayyar spouting nerdiness on *Big Bang Theory* will know exactly what they mean.

31.
Opsimath

noun

A PERSON WHO BEGINS, OR CONTINUES, TO STUDY OR LEARN LATE IN LIFE; ALSO AN OLD STUDENT, A LATE LEARNER

USAGE

When it came to reading, she was definitely an opsimath, as she had never cracked open the cover of a book until she was well past the age of forty.

The word is derived from the Greek words *opsé*, meaning 'late', and *manthánō*, meaning 'learn'. It sounds like a term of approval, but it was not always; for some centuries it carried a connotation of laziness, for an opsimath was one who had waited too long to proceed on the essential path of the acquisition of knowledge. Today there is much more respect for opsimaths, like the remarkable ninety-eight-year-old lady in Kerala who passed her school-leaving examinations last year, having been denied an education by her conservative parents nine decades ago. In the West, 'opsimath clubs' have emerged, hailing such role models as the former American slave Grandma Moses, or for the more classically inclined, Cato the Elder, who learned Greek only at the age of eighty. It is said that the great nineteenth-century French writer Emile Zola was an opsimath who had read the immortal works of Stendhal, Flaubert, Balzac, the Goncourts and Taine, whom French intellectuals of his generation swore by, only late in life, much after his contemporaries.

I have always believed it is never too late to learn; I pride myself on my conviction that I learn something new every day, whether it is a word, a fact, an insight or even a piece of trivia. But to take up an entirely new subject and study it seriously in late adulthood does not come easily. Those who make the effort are well-rewarded. It is said that opsimathy practised by retired people can help ward off dementia and senility, by rejuvenating the synapses in our brains as we learn new things, particularly (but not only) new languages.

In India, adult literacy classes are used to reach out to those, especially women, who were pulled out of school early by misguided (and often unlettered) parents who wanted them to stay at home and help in domestic chores. Such people, who often had no choice in the matter, are happy for the opportunity to resume their studies and acquire such basic skills as being able to read the destination on a bus or the name of a street. You don't have to be mastering Ancient Greek or plasma physics at sixty-five in order to be an opsimath!

32.
Oxymoron

noun

A PHRASE OR FIGURE OF SPEECH IN WHICH
SEEMINGLY CONTRADICTORY TERMS APPEAR IN
CONJUNCTION WITH EACH OTHER

USAGE

Even as he swore to love her for ever, he was looking
around to see if he could do better, but she was taken
in by his falsely true manner.

Oxymorons sound like idiots out of breath gasping for air, but they're just phrases (like 'falsely true' in this example, or 'loving hate' in Shakespeare's *Romeo and Juliet*) that combine two words of opposite meaning to good effect. 'Oxymoron' is derived from the Greek words *oksus*, meaning sharp or pointed, and *moros*, meaning dull or foolish. Of course, for an oxymoron to work, the combined expression has to make sense: there's no point saying 'black white' and expecting people to roar in appreciation, unless you are referring to an African gentleman named Mr White, in which case it's an oxymoron.

Literature is full of oxymorons, the most famous, of course, being Shakespeare's 'Parting is such sweet sorrow'. The immortal P.G. Wodehouse said, 'I always advise people never to give advice.' Irene Peter disregarded this in offering the following advice: 'Always be sincere, even when you don't mean it.' (But then an unknown wag pointed out: 'Free advice is worth what you paid for it.')

Others have also produced oxymora: the movie producer Samuel Goldwyn morosely said, 'If I could drop dead right now, I'd be the happiest man alive.' Paul Fussell found 'nothing more depressing than optimism'. And the author Edna St. Vincent Millay uttered an oxymoronic profundity when she wrote, 'I love humanity, but I hate people.'

In fact, oxymorons are far more common than one might imagine. How often has someone, caught in a place where she shouldn't be, been told to 'act naturally'? How many seemingly knowledgeable people have confided in you an 'open secret'? How often has a clerk demanded an 'original copy'? Or, while negotiating a service, have you demanded an 'exact estimate'? Or said, in a nostalgic conversation, 'I distinctly remember forgetting that.' One might even suggest that 'oxymoron' is a 'typically unusual' term! These are all oxymorons, because if you look at each word, one seems to contradict the other, and yet their meaning is perfectly clear to all of us.

When I was assailed for my use of the expression 'cattle class', I was 'clearly misunderstood'—I had used the term, but it didn't mean what my critics thought it did. When roll-call was taken in a boarding school and a girl was 'found missing', that was an oxymoron as well as a major crisis for the school administration. Boys' boarding schools, of course, feature a lot of conversations about girls, and many of the superficial judgements passed involve oxymorons— 'God, she's pretty ugly', 'she's awfully beautiful', 'that woman was barely dressed', and the like. Girls, being less superficial, are likely to describe the boys they know with other oxymorons: 'he's seriously funny', for instance, or 'he's terribly nice'. Unless, of course, they're clearly confused!

Oxymorons can be deliberate or inadvertent: to speak of a joke being greeted by an audience with 'deafening silence' is an example of the former, whereas a television reporter prattling on about the 'increasing decline' in our employment rate suggests the latter. 'What a "fine mess" you've got us into,' Laurel and Hardy were constantly saying to each other. Most people are 'terribly pleased' to be invited to a picnic where there's a 'definite possibility' that champagne will be served in 'plastic glasses', while they are urged to indulge in 'responsible drinking'. Similarly a young couple spending their quarantine 'alone together', while the woman wears 'loose tights' and they eat 'jumbo shrimps', combines several examples of both kinds.

By their very nature, oxymorons also lend themselves to low humour—when terms that are in fact not contradictory are placed together and described as oxymorons (even when they are not supposed to be), the joke is that you think the expression is a contradiction in terms. 'American culture', some Brits say, is an oxymoron. Some diplomats consider 'United Nations' an oxymoron, since nations are rarely united. A few pseudo-intellectuals list 'military intelligence' as an oxymoron, since they sneer that only the unintelligent go off to risk their lives for the country, or even worse, in another oxymoron, a 'civil war'—for what could be more uncivil than warfare? Of course, when they quit, many soldiers seek an 'active retirement'—another oxymoron. That is, if they hadn't been hit earlier by 'friendly fire'—an oxymoron invented by the military to mask moments of incendiary incompetence. Our public seems to think 'honest politician' is an oxymoron, as is 'business ethics'; they also laugh at 'educational television' as a misnomer. Many an anti-romantic would claim 'Happily Married' is an oxymoron . . .

The recent 'social distancing measures' in India prompted several of us to treat each day as a 'working holiday'. Some, stuck in confinement, were inclined to let out a 'silent scream'. Of course, if they violate the curfew, the government made it clear they will respond with a 'zero tolerance' policy.

One can sometimes stretch an oxymoron beyond a two-word phrase to an idea. Only Donald Trump, of course, could speak of exceeding an 'unlimited budget'. At the other end of the moral scale, Sarojini Naidu said of Mahatma Gandhi, 'If only he knew how much it costs us to keep him in poverty!' Sam Goldwyn came up with several of these longer oxymora: 'Anyone who goes to a psychiatrist ought to have his head examined' was the best, though 'A verbal contract isn't worth the paper it's written on' is the best-known. And what about the wit who said, 'Thank God I'm an atheist!'?

Finally, ask frustrated computer users to nominate an oxymoron from their daily experience, and many will suggest 'Microsoft Works'. Does it work for you?

33.
Pandemic

adjective and noun

RELATING TO A DISEASE AFFECTING A WHOLE
PEOPLE OR REGION, USUALLY THE WHOLE
WORLD; ANY CONTAGION THAT SPREADS
THROUGHOUT AN ENTIRE POPULATION,
COUNTRY, OR THE GLOBE, CROSSING
INTERNATIONAL BOUNDARIES

USAGE

The World Health Organisation declared COVID-19 a
global pandemic, thus distinguishing it from an epidemic,
which would have occurred in a smaller region.

The word pandemic is derived from the Greek *pandemos*, meaning 'pertaining to all people; public, common', in turn made up of *pan* ('all') and *demos* ('people'). An epidemic spreads rapidly and extensively by infection, but a pandemic threatens everyone, not just in a limited region, and causes a high level of mortality. So the Ebola virus, though it killed thousands of people, remained confined to West Africa and never reached pandemic status. And when what we today know as COVID-19 seemed to be confined to China, experts spoke of it as an epidemic; when it crossed borders and affected all countries, the WHO labelled it a pandemic.

Coronavirus is by no means the only pandemic the world has had to cope with. Influenza has often reached pandemic proportions, most notoriously in 1918–19, when the misnamed 'Spanish flu' killed more people around the world than both World Wars combined! There have been several lethal pandemics of flu—one million died in the 'Russian flu' in 1889–90, the 'Asian Flu' killed 2 million in 1956–58, and the 'Hong Kong Flu' accounted for 1 million fatalities in 1968. There have been alerts in recent years about avian or bird flu, swine flu, the 2003 severe acute respiratory syndrome (SARS), and other threats of pandemics that have placed the world on high alert.

Cholera, bubonic plague and smallpox have produced deadly pandemics in the past. None, perhaps, has been as persistent, devastating and recurrent as smallpox, which killed between 300 to 500 million people in its 12,000-year existence—a much higher proportion of the world population in earlier times—and whose eradication by the 1970s is one of the truly great medical achievements of humankind.

HIV/AIDS, because it spread around the world and caused 36 million fatalities since 1981, can be called a pandemic. Cholera no longer is thought of as a contender, but what is known as the Sixth Cholera Pandemic was: it originated in India where it killed over 800,000, before spreading to the Middle East, North Africa, Eastern Europe and even the USA, where it caused the last American outbreak of cholera in 1910–1911.

The most feared pandemic scourge of humanity in ancient and mediaeval times was, of course, the Plague. The Bubonic Plague of 1346–53 lasted seven years and killed an incredible 75–200 million people, out of a world population perhaps three times that size. It ravaged Europe, Africa and Asia, travelling around the world most probably on rat-infested merchant ships. Its toll was so widespread and horrific that it was known as the 'Black Death'. But there had been earlier bubonic plagues, though labelling them pandemics might suggest a certain European ethnocentricity, since Europe was all that people knew of the world in those days. The 'Plague of Justinian' in 541–42 AD wiped out some 25 million people, which was half the population of Europe, killed up to a quarter of the population of the Eastern Mediterranean and devastated the city of Constantinople, where 40 per cent of the population died. Even earlier, in 165 AD, the 'Plague of Galen', also known as the 'Antonine Plague', affected Asia Minor, Egypt, Greece and Italy. Historians attempting to understand what happened surmise that it must have been either smallpox or measles, brought back to Rome by soldiers returning from battle in Mesopotamia. Whatever it was, this plague killed over 5 million people and decimated the Roman army.

Pandemics, of course, have become more frequent in our times because of increased global travel and integration, population growth and environmental damage. The increasing emergence of viral disease from animals, whether because of the eating habits of some humans or as a result of environmental deformations, has seen an increase in zoonotic diseases, in which pathogens cross the boundary between animal-to-animal transmission and affect human beings as well by transforming into diseases that are transmitted from human to human.

Pandemics cause significant economic, social and political disruption, prompting the international community, notably through the World Health Organisation, to undertake efforts to prepare to mitigate the impact of pandemics. There are still many gaps and shortfalls related to the timely detection of disease, availability of basic care, tracing of the spread of infection, the quarantine and isolation procedures adopted by various countries, and major challenges of global coordination and response, as well as the mobilization of resources to fight pandemics, particularly in poor developing countries.

The worst pandemic threats are those that transmit easily and rapidly between humans, have long asymptomatic infectious periods (which means that infected persons can infect others while their infections are still undetected), and are easily confused with lesser threats (a cold or a flu, for instance, in the case of COVID-19). Others, like Nipah virus and bird flu, are deemed a moderate global threat since they have not demonstrated sustained human-to-human transmission. Developing countries are always the most at risk, because of their higher levels of malnutrition, insufficient access to good medical care and higher rates of disease transmission, as well as lower medical infrastructure capacity, less access to modern medical techniques and greater density of population.

The world is going through a severe pandemic right now in 2020, in which relatively developed countries seem to be the worst sufferers. We will have to wait and see if that remains the case for long, and what lessons we must derive from it.

34.
Panglossian

adjective

FOOLISHLY AND UNREALISTICALLY OPTIMISTIC, ESPECIALLY IN THE FACE OF UNRELIEVED HARDSHIP OR ADVERSITY

———

USAGE

'Ayushman Bharat' is essentially a Panglossian idea, a policy based on wishful thinking.

Panglossian is derived from Pangloss, an incurably optimistic character who was a philosopher and tutor in Voltaire's 1758 work *Candide*, and who famously declared that 'all is for the best in this best of all possible worlds'.

Voltaire clearly did not intend us to be enamoured of this approach, since Dr Pangloss was old, pedantic and deluded, maintaining his misguided beliefs even after experiencing great suffering. His name itself is a clue to the playwright's view of the old man, since Pangloss is derived from the Greek *pan*, all, and *glossa*, tongue or language, so suggesting empty talk or shallow glibness.

In India, the ruling party spokesmen are obliged to be professional Panglossians, putting the finest spin even on the most unsavoury acts of the government, seeing a glowing silver lining in every economic or political cloud. It is impossible to get an official voice to ever acknowledge how bad things actually are; they will tell you they are actually fine, good and heading irresistibly for better.

It is hard to escape using this word when one reads the Modi government's embarrassing attempts to positively gloss every misfortune currently afflicting our nation. To respond to the healthcare crisis confronting the least fortunate sections of Indian society by announcing an insurance scheme that covers the entire population only for the most routine maladies, and budgets a fraction of a percentage of what the scheme will actually cost if all the sick laid claim to benefits under it, is Panglossian in the extreme. So is suggesting that, just as the Mahabharata war was won in eighteen days, the war against the coronavirus would be won in twenty-one (as the PM did when the first lockdown was announced).

The recent coronavirus crisis witnessed more Panglossians in the governmental ranks: several first assured us there was no problem, that Indians were immune to the virus and that the summer heat would destroy the contagion if they weren't. When this turned out not to be true, the line changed to how masterfully the government had handled the crisis and how India—despite manifest inadequacies of testing, unavailability of equipment from ventilators to protective gear for healthcare professionals, poor hospital facilities and a faltering economy ill-prepared to buffer the shocks endured by businesses and workers—would triumph easily over the crisis. Many announcements by the government about 'flattening the curve' looked decidedly Panglossian when the curve continued to climb three months into the lockdown. Clapping and banging plates at 5 p.m. signalled our optimism, and our premature triumphalism. As the numbers passed the half-million mark with no sign of the crisis easing or the 'peak' having been reached, and as a prominent businessman looked at the economic indicators and declared, 'we flattened the wrong curve', it became clear that a lot of the earlier official projections were Panglossian indeed.

Some professions require chronic Panglossians. Public relations and marketing are two fields that lend themselves to such behaviour: no one sells a product, or promotes a project or a company, by expressing gloom about its prospects, even when these seem dire to external observers. Sports is another such domain: captains and coaches are perennially Panglossian about their teams' chances, even when they have just been comprehensively thrashed in their previous match. 'We will win the next game,' they bravely and confidently boast, even if no one else on the planet believes they have a hope in hell of doing so.

Armies are the same: victory is always declared to be imminent, if only to keep up the morale of the troops on the front. George Orwell wrote movingly of how, in the Spanish Civil War, the Republican troops besieging the city of Huesca were told, 'We'll be home for Christmas.' That proved Panglossian: Huesca never fell, and the only Republican soldiers who made it home did so on a stretcher, or in a coffin.

35.
Paracosm

noun

A DETAILED IMAGINARY WORLD CREATED
INSIDE ONE'S MIND

———

USAGE

My little daughter spent much of her hours not merely
daydreaming but conducting entire conversations
and incidents in her own paracosm, with people
and pets only she could see.

Derived from Ancient Greek *pará* ('beside, alongside') and *kósmos* ('world, universe'), paracosms are more common among imaginative children than you can imagine. A paracosm is defined as a detailed imaginary or fantasy world, involving humans, animals, or imaginary creatures, often having its own geography, history and language, usually created and developed during childhood. As a child, sharing a bathtub with my toddler sisters, I used to invent a paracosm for the three of us and regale them with stories of adventures therein. As they grew older, I would pause in mid-story and challenge them to pick up where I had left off, so the story was completed collectively. Adults tend to outgrow their paracosms, but some cling on to them, for psychological and personal reasons.

So it is not only novelists like J.R.R. Tolkien in his *Lord of the Rings* or J.K. Rowling in her Harry Potter books who have created convincing imaginary worlds peopled with their own characters, clans (Tolkien's Hobbits, Rowling's Muggles), traditions, geographical features, historical events, invented language and even habits and prejudices—including, in some cases, incorporating real-world characters and conventions. Many ordinary individuals without any literary talent have created them too.

A child's imaginary paracosm is very real to her, and she has a profound and complex relationship with it; one friend's son claimed his best friend was a girl who for the rest of us didn't exist, but he spoke of her as if he was completely serious about his accounts of exchanges and experiences they had shared. Though adults are often bewildered by the conviction a child shows in her subjective universe, it can often continue beyond childhood.

Paracosms are not merely infantile fantasies, as the successes of Tolkien, Rowling, the *Game of Thrones* series on television and lesser-known children's authors confirm. They often serve for grieving people to cope with tragedy, especially the death of a loved one, when bereaved people retreat into a paracosm in order to more safely process and understand their loss. It is said that famous writers like Emily Bronte, James M. Barrie and Isak Dinesen created their widely-read paracosms after the deaths in their childhoods of family members who were close to them. Children invent paracosms as a way of orienting themselves in reality, never more essential than when their reality has undergone the shock of a bereavement or major loss. The Oscar-winning 2006 Spanish film *Pan's Labyrinth* beautifully depicts the paracosm inhabited by a young schoolgirl whose father is killed in the Civil War and whose mother marries a fascist officer.

Today, one of the best-loved paracosms is the one inhabited by the cartoon strip characters Calvin and Hobbes—a little boy coping with the stresses of daily life, parental instructions and onerous demands of the real world by talking to, and receiving support from, a friendly tiger.

Sometimes we wonder whether some of our politicians live in paracosms of their own—how else to explain some of their more bizarre decisions and actions?

36.
Paraprosdokian

noun

A FIGURE OF SPEECH IN WHICH THE LATTER PART OF A SENTENCE OR PHRASE, OR LARGER STATEMENT, IS SURPRISING OR UNEXPECTED, IN A WAY THAT PROMPTS THE READER OR HEARER TO RETHINK THE FIRST PART OR UNDERSTAND IT DIFFERENTLY

USAGE

My favourite paraprosdokian declares that 'the pun is the lowest form of humour—when you don't think of it first'.

Paraprosdokian comes from two Greek words, *para*, meaning 'against', and *prosdokia*, meaning 'expectation'. The earliest citation in English seems to be in 1891 in a humorous article in *Punch*: 'A "paraprosdokian", which delights him to the point of repetition.' It is frequently used for humorous or dramatic effect— 'I want to die peacefully in my sleep like my father, not screaming and terrified like his passengers' was a famous paraprosdokian of the comedian Bob Monkhouse. Groucho Marx loved using it for its anti-climaxes: 'I've had a perfectly wonderful evening, but this wasn't it.' I forget who said 'The last thing I want to do is hurt you, but it's still on the list'.

Paraprosdokians are particularly popular among stand-up comedians: 'When I was ten, I beat up the school bully. His arms were in casts. That's what gave me the courage.' Or 'I asked God for a bike, but I know God doesn't work that way, so I stole a bike and asked for forgiveness.' One old favourite is: 'Change is inevitable, except from a vending machine.' And how about 'Always borrow money from a pessimist. He won't expect it back!'?

Satirists can excel at paraprosdokians: what better way to skewer the pretensions of society? 'She got her good looks from her father; he's a plastic surgeon.' Or more notoriously: 'I can picture in my mind a world without war, a world without hate. And I can picture us attacking that world, because they'd never expect it.' Cuttingly: 'When tempted to fight fire with fire, remember that the fire department usually uses water.' Memorably: 'Going to a temple doesn't make you a Hindu any more than standing in a garage makes you a car.'

A good use of paraprosdokians is to send up the conventional wisdom people like to inflict on you. 'I always take life with a grain of salt—plus a slice of lemon, and a shot of tequila.' Or 'To steal ideas from one person is plagiarism. To steal from many is research.'

Some paraprosdokians not only change the meaning of the first part of an observation, but they also play on the meaning of a particular word, creating a double joke: 'War does not determine who is right—only who is left.' Or 'I used to be indecisive. Now I'm not sure.' I'm still awed by the brilliance of 'Nostalgia isn't what it used to be'.

Perhaps the greatest craftsman of paraprosdokians was the immortal P.G. Wodehouse. A mere sentence was not enough for him; his best examples built up slowly and at length. 'Myrtle Prosser was a woman of considerable but extremely severe beauty. She . . . suggested rather one of those engravings of the mistresses of Bourbon kings which make one feel that the monarchs who selected them must have been men of iron, impervious to fear—or else short-sighted.'

And that's probably enough paraprosdokians. After all, a bus station is where a bus stops. A train station is where a train stops. On my desk, I have a work station . . .

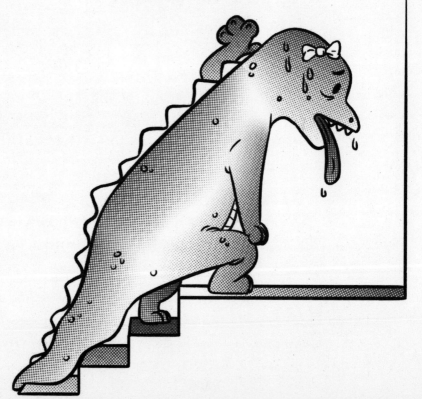

37.
Phobia

noun

AN EXTREME DISLIKE OR IRRATIONAL FEAR OF, OR AVERSION TO, SOMETHING, WHETHER A PLACE, A SITUATION OR AN ANIMAL

———

USAGE

She can never get into a crowded lift because she suffers from claustrophobia.

ALSO

He lives alone in the mountains because he has a phobia about crowds and freaks out with a bad case of ochlophobia every time he comes into the city.

As these examples suggest, phobias come in various shapes and sizes. The word itself derives from the Greek—phobia, from *phobos*, meaning 'fear, panic fear, terror, outward show of fear; object of fear or terror', though originally it meant 'flight', in the sense of fleeing, which was how the epic poet Homer used the word. (That too conceals an interesting story: phobia traces its origins to the Proto-Indo-European root word *bhegw-*, meaning 'to run', which of course has survived in Hindi as 'bhaag' and 'bhagna'.)

Phobias involve fear of various sorts: there's fear of creatures or things, from spiders and rats to needles or mirrors. There's the fear of certain situations, from riding a car or a lift to being caught in a storm. There's social phobias, from fear of untidiness to fear of eating in public. There are the more 'understandable' nervous fears, of blood, or dentists, or heights. All of them, in severe cases, can involve attacks of anxiety or panic, racing heartbeats, sweating, palpitations, nausea and the risk of fainting. In other words, phobias are not to be taken lightly.

The better-known phobias include *claustrophobia*, a fear of closed spaces, and its opposite, *agoraphobia*, an aversion to wide open spaces. There's *acrophobia*, a fear of heights (from the same root that gives us the word 'acrobat' for a high-flying trapeze artist or tightrope-walker), *arachnophobia* (a fear of spiders, a surprisingly common phobia amongst women) and the condition mentioned in our second usage example, *ochlophobia*, a fear of crowds. Most common of all is *xenophobia*, an aversion to strangers, and a widespread affliction in the Western world these days, as well as increasingly seen, sadly, in BJP-ruled India.

Less common as words, but not as conditions, is *aerophobia*, a fear of flying (I was once seated on a flight next to a very pretty actress who suffered from aerophobia and asked me to hold her hand tightly during take-off, landing and every time the plane hit turbulence, which got me some arch looks from the stewardesses and fellow passengers!), *amathophobia*, an aversion to dust (I am a mild sufferer from this condition myself), *haematophobia*, a fear of blood (which puts many students off biology when they first have to perform a dissection!) and *nyctophobia*, a fear of the dark (how many children do you know who *don't* suffer from nyctophobia?)

Then there are the really rare and obscure conditions for which words nonetheless exist, like *ereuthophobia*, the fear of blushing, *emetophobia*, a fear of vomiting (pity the poor emetophobe who becomes pregnant!), *ornithophobia* (the fear of birds) and its cousin *zoophobia* (aversion to animals). (An extreme version of the latter is *alektorophobia*, fear of chickens!) Schoolchildren might suffer from *scolionophobia*, the fear of school, though their teachers might be victims of *ephebiphobia* (the fear of teenagers: met any terrifying ones lately?)

There are words you imagine should be in more common use than they are, like *pyrophobia* (the fear of fire), *verminophobia* (the fear of germs) and *triskadekaphobia*, fear of the number thirteen, a widespread affliction of the superstitious. As a child I lived in a building in Kolkata that had a twelfth floor and then a fourteenth floor but no thirteenth, for fear people would deem it unlucky and refuse to live there.

Some terms for phobias are quixotic: *keraunophobia* sounds like an aversion to the chief minister of Kerala (the Kera Uno!) but is actually the word for a fear of thunder, which we hear a lot in Kerala, particularly preceding pre-monsoon showers. Since Keralites are warm people, they may be more susceptible to *cryophobia*, fear of ice or cold.

All phobias, doctors tell us, are more common in women. (That includes *androphobia*, the fear of men, which may also be linked to *aphenphosmphobia*, the fear of being touched—especially by a man with facial hair, if you are suffering from *pogonophobia*, the fear of beards.) Among particularly female conditions are *cacophobia*, the fear of ugliness, *obesophobia*, the fear of gaining weight, *ataxophobia*, the fear of disorder or untidiness, *atelophobia*, the fear of imperfection, and *catagelophobia*, the fear of being ridiculed.

Phobias affect one in every eight people around the world, so we need to take them seriously. Still, the one condition no male of my acquaintance has ever admitted to—even those suffering from *gamophobia*, the fear of marriage, or *venustraphobia*, the fear of beautiful women—is *genophobia*, a fear of sex. Given the trolling I have become accustomed to, I should stop here: this long but still-partial list is enough to give many readers *phobophobia*—a phobia about phobias!

38.
Prepone

verb

TO ADVANCE AN APPOINTMENT OR PLAN;
TO MOVE FORWARD IN TIME

———

USAGE

The traffic was much lighter than we had expected, so I
called my host to ask if we could prepone our meeting.

I have long immodestly considered myself the inventor of the term 'prepone'. I came up with it at St. Stephen's in 1972, used it extensively in conversation and employed it in an article in *JS* magazine soon after. 'Prepone', as a back-construction from 'postpone', seemed so much simpler, to a teenage collegian, than clunkily saying 'could you move that appointment earlier?' or 'I would like to advance that deadline' or 'please bring it forward to an earlier date'. Over the years, I was gratified to see how extensively its use had spread in India.

But boy, was I wrong. In keeping with the long-standing wisdom that there is nothing new under the sun, I am told by Catherine Henstridge of the *Oxford English Dictionary*, no less, that they have an example of the use of the word 'prepone' from 1913—and it is not, alas, Indian.

In 1913, a J.J.D. Trenor wrote in the *New York Times*: 'May I be permitted to coin the word "prepone" as a needed rival of that much revered and oft-invoked standby, "postpone"?' It didn't catch on much in the West, but the proceedings of the 1952 Indian Science Congress reveal that other Indians thought along the same lines: 'In Indian villages . . . demand for power can be preponed or postponed not only by hours but even by days in order to comply with meteorological conditions.'

Clearly, the origin of 'prepone' has been preponed from 1972 to 1913, and I duly withdraw my claim to its origination. Mind you, I can still make a case, through frequent usage, to being somewhat involved in its popularization!

Still, the persistence and survival of what is called 'Indian English' (often with a sneer, as if to differentiate it from the Queen's 'propah' English) deserves to be taken seriously. Our English, spoken without the shadow of Englishmen looming over us, is a vigorous and local language, which draws strength from local roots. If Americans can say 'fall' for autumn and 'gotten' for 'have got', though both are archaisms in England itself, why can't Indians say 'furlong', 'fortnight' and 'do the needful', even if these have fallen out of use centuries ago in London? So many words in Indian English have stood up to the only test that matters—the test of time and usage. If enough people find a word or phrase useful, it is, to my mind, legitimate.

Indian English is a living, practical language, used by millions every day for practical purposes. Many phrases we take for granted in ordinary conversation are actually quite unusual abroad—calling elders 'auntie' or 'uncle', for instance, or using the expression 'non-veg' to convey a willingness to eat meat. That doesn't make them wrong, or even quaint. It just makes them Indian.

Some Indian English was created by our media and passed into regular usage— 'airdash' ('the chief minister airdashed to Delhi') and 'history sheeter' ('the police explained that habitual criminal X was a history sheeter', i.e., that he had a long criminal record). Some, like my 'prepone', came from school and college campuses: 'mugging' (cramming hard for an exam, with much rote learning and memorization involved) uses a word that means two very different things abroad (a criminal assault by a robber, as in 'She was the victim of a mugging in a dark alley' or an elaborate and often comically exaggerated expression, as in 'he was mugging for the camera'). When an Indian student tells a foreigner he was 'mugging for an exam', bewilderment is guaranteed. Yet it's a vivid word that conveys exactly what is intended to every user of Indian English.

Some Indian Englishisms are merely translated from an Indian language: 'what is your good name?' is the classic, since all Bengalis have a '*daak naam*' that they are called by, and a '*bhalo naam*' (or 'good name') for the record. But 'what is your good name?' is still the most polite form, in any Indian version of the English language, for finding out the identity of your interlocutor.

Some Indianisms are creative uses of an ordinary English word or phrase to reflect a particularly Indian sensibility—such as 'kindly adjust', said apologetically by the seventh person slipping into a bench meant for four. Our matrimonial ads have created their own cultural tropes with expressions that only mean something in Indian English—'wheatish complexion', of course, and better still, 'traditional with modern outlook'.

But acknowledging the legitimacy of Indian English and many of its formulations doesn't mean that 'anything goes'. Some things are simply wrong. The Indian habit of saying 'I will return back' is an unnecessary redundancy: if you return, you are coming back. The desi practice of using 'till' to mean 'as long as' is simply incorrect English; it is wrong to say 'I will miss you till you are away' when you really mean is 'I will miss you till you come back'! The Indian official doesn't 'waive off' a fine, he just waives it, though he could wave you off if you thank him too profusely. 'I am staying Bandra side' is not an acceptable equivalent of 'I am living in the Bandra area'. And 'back side' for 'rear' causes much unwitting hilarity, as in signs proclaiming, 'entry through back side only'. These can't be justified under the rubric of Indian English. They are just bad English.

But for the rest, we have nothing to apologize about: we should defiantly celebrate their use as integral parts of our Indian English vocabulary. After all, 'we are like that only'. And if you don't like it, kindly adjust . . .

39.
Quarantine

noun and verb

A PERIOD OF ENFORCED ISOLATION FOR A
PERSON, ANIMAL, OR OBJECT SUSPECTED OF
CARRYING A COMMUNICABLE DISEASE

———

USAGE

All the passengers on the cruise ship *Diamond Princess*
were placed in quarantine for fear they might have been
infected by the coronavirus.

The pandemic of novel coronavirus (COVID-19) assailing the world has suddenly brought the word 'quarantine' into widespread use. The term goes back to the 1660s, when disease was often carried across the seas on ships, and referred to the period a ship suspected of carrying disease was kept in isolation. Quarantine came from the Italian *quarantinagiorni*, literally 'space of forty days,' from *quaranta* (forty) and *giorni* (days), in keeping with the Venetian policy (first enforced in 1377) of keeping ships from plague-stricken countries waiting off its port for forty days to assure that no communicable cases were aboard, since no effective treatment or cure was known then. After three centuries of this practice in Italy, the broader sense of 'any period of forced isolation' emerged.

Initially, the Venetians reacted to the bubonic plague, known notoriously as the Black Death, which was spreading through Europe between 1347 and 1350 (it is estimated that one-third of Europe's population died). The Great Council of Ragusa passed a law establishing *trentino*, or a thirty-day period of isolation for ships arriving from plague-affected areas. When in 1377 the isolation period was extended from thirty to forty days, the term changed from *trentino* to quarantino.

Interestingly, in English the word quarantine had an earlier meaning, that of a period of forty days in which a widow had the right (and some say, the obligation) to remain in her dead husband's house (1520s), and even earlier, as quarentyne, it had religious connotations, referring to the time in the desert in which Christ fasted for forty days, Moses' time on Mount Sinai, and the Catholic observation of Lent, a forty-day period of spiritual purification. Now its usage is perhaps more common and more banal, as in, 'My dog had to be quarantined when I moved back to India.' Indian students evacuated from the Wuhan area were 'in quarantine' in Manesar, along with the brave diplomats (one of them a nephew of mine) who went to arrange their evacuation.

When an outbreak of SARS moved through Canada in 2003, about 30,000 people in Toronto were quarantined. Epidemiologists (experts in the spread of disease) are still debating whether it effectively helped to control the spread of disease, but in any case, during the 2014 Ebola outbreak in West Africa, health workers returning to the United States from affected areas were quarantined.

The aim of quarantine is to prevent transmission of the disease from potentially infected persons to healthy persons during the incubation period. Quarantine can take two forms: absolute or complete quarantine, which consists of a limitation of freedom for a period equal to the longest usual incubation period of the disease; and modified quarantine, which involves selective or partial limitation of movement, such as the exclusion of children from school or the confining of military personnel to their base. It therefore involves infringing upon the liberty of outwardly healthy people, and this has both legal and ethical implications which should not be taken lightly.

Few infectious diseases have an incubation time or infective period greater than forty days—except rabies, which may not show up for several months. That is why animals that may have been exposed to rabies are quarantined for many months when they arrive in other countries. HIV (human immunodeficiency virus) does have a longer incubation period than SARS or COVID-19, but human rights advocates have ensured there is no quarantine for potential carriers of that infection, which in any case cannot be spread as easily as SARS or COVID-19.

In 1969, the World Health Organisation issued international health regulations for just four designated quarantinable diseases: cholera, plague, yellow fever and smallpox. Smallpox was proclaimed eradicated by the WHO in 1979, and the other diseases on the list are relatively rare, so the quarantine stations that were formerly common in many seaports around the world have been abandoned, taken down, or converted into holiday resorts.

Quarantine law and regulations still apply in many countries, however, to protect animals and plants of economic importance from exotic diseases. Animal and plant quarantine procedures are often as important as human quarantine. The economic importance of agriculture and animal husbandry in many countries makes it vital for them to keep out diseases that might wipe out valuable cattle herds or destroy a season's harvest.

Quarantine is usually always used literally, but that doesn't prevent us from applying the word metaphorically, as in: 'I would love to quarantine his bigoted communal ideas to prevent them infecting more people.'

40.
Quiz

noun and verb

BRIEF EXAMINATION OF
A STUDENT ON SOME SUBJECT

USAGE

It's always amazing that Indian students, who have to undergo so many tests and exams, still seem to enjoy participating in a quiz.

The origin of the word 'quiz' is obscure: its first use, in the late 1700s, was to refer to an oddball or eccentric person (as the *London Magazine* put it, 'one who thinks, speaks, or acts differently from the rest of the world in general'). Since it was also used for people who were pedantic and rule-bound, it was the late-eighteenth-century equivalent of calling someone a 'nerd' or a 'dweeb'. Later it became another word for a joke or a wisecrack. It's only in the last century and a half that it has been used in the current sense, of a set of questions requiring short answers.

One marvellous story attributes it to the manager of the Theatre Royal in the capital of Ireland, Dublin, named either Richard Daly or James Daly (depending on which version you trust), who apparently bet that he could create a new word without any meaning and have everybody in the city using it within forty-eight hours. Challenged to prove this, he allegedly employed a large number of street-children (the Brits and Irish called them urchins in those days) to go around the city and chalk the word 'quiz' on every surface they could find—doors, windows and walls—so that the next day everybody was asking what this strange word meant. The word was short enough and easy enough for the urchins to write and people to remember it, and Daly accordingly won his bet, bringing 'quiz' into popular usage. Many linguists express scepticism about this story, suspecting a newspaper editor simply invented it to pad his columns, but I love the sound of it. Not every word comes with such a good story attached!

The *Oxford Dictionary* tells us that 'the word is nevertheless hard to account for, and so is its later meaning of "to question or interrogate". This emerged in the mid-nineteenth century and gave rise to the most common use of the term today, for a type of entertainment based on a test of a person's knowledge.' The 1971 edition of the *Oxford English Dictionary* suggests that its current meaning may be derived from the second syllable of the word 'inquisitive', which in turn derives from the Latin *inquirire* (to inquire). That certainly is more plausible than the Daly tall-tale.

Today we all know that a quiz is a form of mind game, in which the players (as individuals or in teams) attempt to answer questions correctly to demonstrate their knowledge—either about a certain subject (like a 'literature quiz') or of esoteric and otherwise useless trivia (a 'general knowledge' quiz). Indians love to reveal their mastery of GK, and quiz competitions are a staple of most interschool and intercollegiate contests, sometimes televised to large audiences and increasingly featuring generous prizes. I was a 'quizard' in my college days, a term I invented, and proudly number, among my most cherished extracurricular achievements, founding the St. Stephen's College Quiz Club in 1974 and serving as its first president. In those days it was the first such quiz club in the country; today rare is the college that doesn't have one.

Quizzing has also evolved considerably since I was a contestant in them, having become more sophisticated and complicated through the use of visual and musical questions, obscure slides and videos, and trick questions. But while in India we know of quizzes essentially as a sport (and watch them purely for entertainment), in some countries, notably the United States and Canada, a quiz is a serious educational challenge. The word is used for a form of student assessment that has fewer questions, usually of less difficulty, and requires less time for completion, than a test or examination. It's often resorted to in classrooms to quickly check comprehension of a new lesson. In the US you also hear of a 'pop quiz', in which students are given no time to prepare but are simply surprised with it in class to see if they are up to speed with what is being taught.

But quizzes have acquired worldwide fame and popularity principally as money-spinners for gifted housewives on television shows, most famously *Who Wants to be a Millionaire?* and its spinoffs. *Kaun Banega Crorepati*, one may well ask—and the real answer is the well-paid TV quizmaster!

41.
Rodomontade

noun, verb and adjective

BOASTFUL OR INFLATED TALK OR BEHAVIOUR

———

USAGE

The politician's rodomontade speeches sought to conceal his total lack of substance, or indeed of any real accomplishment.

Rodomontade is a delightful word, as swaggeringly self-important as the behaviour it seeks to describe. It originated in the late sixteenth century as a reference to Rodomonte, the Saracen king of Algiers, a character in both the 1495 poem *Orlando Innamorato* by Count M.M. Boiardo, and its sequel, Ludovico Ariosto's 1516 Italian romantic epic *Orlando Furioso*, who was much given to vain boasting. I am told the name was inspired by an Italian dialect in which the word literally means 'one who rolls (away) the mountain'. In English, it was used to describe an extravagant braggart.

There's a line from a John Donne poem from 1612, 'Challengers cartells, full of Rodomontades', that suggests that a rodomontade is a single boast that can be multiplied in the plural, but modern usage dispenses with the 's', using rodomontade as a collective noun for an entirely boastful disposition, bombastic language or empty bragging. Literature students might recall this lovely usage in the nineteenth-century novel *The Tenant of Wildfell Hall* by Anne Brontë: 'She knows what she's about; but he, poor fool, deludes himself with the notion that she'll make him a good wife, and because she has amused him with some rodomontade about despising rank and wealth in matters of love and marriage, he flatters himself that she's devotedly attached to him.'

Inevitably, the word has been used for politicians—one can deliver a speech that is an 'empty rodomontade, a string of resounding sentiments aiming not at conviction but at applause'. Or one can use it to describe the style of President Donald Trump, who is much given to extolling himself in the most unselfconsciously boastful terms ('No one knows more about this than me', he has said, and 'I'm the greatest'.)

The word was applied to the rhetorical style of a very different man, too, the boxing champ Muhammad Ali. One newspaper article writes: 'Until the mid-'60s, rodomontade was rare even in sports. Then came Muhammad Ali. His exuberant braggadocio was what made Ali so different . . .'. As the Ali example suggests, rodomontade is not confined only to politicians: the *Oxford English Dictionary* cites a 1919 usage to characterize society in general—'These instances in themselves are not edifying to our rodomontade civilization.'

Rodomontade, by extension, can even apply to music full of pomp and flourishes. The German composer Georg Philipp Telemann composed a Suite in H minor for violin solo and strings which ends with a piece named 'Rodomontade'. The singer Morrissey has described his own music as rodomontade. It is less used in literature, unless one is being distinctly uncomplimentary. Vladimir Nabokov criticized Fyodor Dostoevsky for his 'gothic rodomontade'.

Still, politicians are more given to rodomontade than most, and no better example can be found than that of the braggadocious Winston Churchill, whose wartime Foreign Secretary, Lord Halifax, found him impossible to work with. A senior bureaucrat with the Foreign Office, Alexander Cadogan, counselling his boss, was reported to have said: 'His rodomontades probably bore you as much as they do me, but don't do anything silly under the stress of that.' (The plural crept in as late as 1940, and in written accounts of this exchange there is an extra 'h' in the spelling, rhodomontade, which is definitely not the preferred style today.) Even Roy Jenkins in his adulatory biography of Churchill wrote of a general who 'revealed a plain soldier's distaste for the publicity rodomontade which always attended Churchill'.

Churchill's adversaries, the Nazis, were no better. The great chronicler of the worst war crimes of that era, Hannah Arendt, in her book *Eichmann in Jerusalem*, describes Adolf Eichmann's boasting: 'Bragging was the vice that was Eichmann's undoing. It was sheer rodomontade when he told men working under him during the last days of the war: "I will jump into my grave laughing, because the fact that I have the death of five million Jews . . . on my conscience gives me extraordinary satisfaction."'

In my UN days, the Falklands War of 1982 led to strongly critical attacks in the UN Security Council on Britain as a colonial power imposing its military will on Argentina. The UK ambassador, Sir Anthony Parsons, began his response to the Security Council debate by saying: 'Obviously we expected other delegations to give bent to atrociously offensive, confused and ill-directed rodomontades against my country . . .'

On the whole, then, rodomontade is best avoided; simple language is always preferred. After all, the character Rodomonte's extravagantly boastful talk in the epic leads to his death. Speak modestly, and you can stay alive!

42.
Satyagraha

noun

AN ACT OF NON-VIOLENT CIVIL RESISTANCE,
A TERM INVENTED BY MAHATMA GANDHI

USAGE

Mahatma Gandhi first resorted to satyagraha during his
early battles in South Africa, though the concept gained
recognition and respect when he applied it to the freedom
struggle in India.

The Mahatma invented the term satyagraha—literally, 'holding on to truth' or, as Gandhiji variously described it, truth-force, love force or soul-force—to describe his method of action in terms that also imbued it with moral content and authority. He called satyagraha a 'religious movement': 'It is a process of purification and penance. It seeks to secure reforms or redress of grievances by self-suffering.'

In his own words, 'The pursuit of truth did not admit of violence being inflicted on one's opponent but that he must be weaned from error by patience and compassion. For what appears to be truth to the one may appear to be error to the other. And patience means self-suffering. So the doctrine came to mean vindication of truth, not by infliction of suffering on the opponent, but on oneself.' Thus when he first called for a fast, Gandhiji was at pains to stress it was not in the nature of a 'hunger-strike, or as designed to put any pressure upon the Government'. It was instead, 'for all satyagrahis, the necessary discipline to fit them for the civil disobedience contemplated in their Pledge, and for all others, some slight token of the intensity of their wounded feelings'. The satyagrahi's objective, according to the Mahatma, was 'to convert, not to coerce, the wrong-doer'.

Gandhiji conceived the term 'satyagraha'—a compound of two Sanskrit words, satya, meaning truth, and āgraha, connoting 'polite insistence' or 'holding firmly to'—in South Africa after a public competition in 1906. He disliked the English term 'passive resistance', which journalists had applied to his civil disobedience movement, because satyagraha required activism, not passivity. If you believed in Truth and cared enough to obtain it, Gandhiji felt, you could not afford to be passive: you had to be prepared actively to suffer for Truth.

No dictionary imbues 'truth' with the depth of meaning Gandhiji gave it. His truth emerged from his convictions: it meant not only what was accurate, but what was just and therefore right. Truth could not be obtained by 'untruthful' or unjust means, which included inflicting violence upon one's opponent. 'I believe that non-violence is infinitely superior to violence, forgiveness is more manly than punishment.' Hence, he would call off a satyagraha if any participant resorted to violence—as he did when the killing of policemen in Chauri Chaura in 1922 led him to call off his nationwide protests just as they were gathering steam.

Satya is derived from the word 'sat', or 'being'; Truth is that which exists, and there is no reality beyond Truth. For Gandhiji, Truth encompassed all aspects of being, from truthfulness in speech and a refusal to lie, to an acknowledgement of the immanence of real truth, as opposed to what is non-existent (asat). In moral terms he saw the Truth he was striving to hold to as the defence of the good as opposed to evil; he had no hesitation in telling the British viceroy that he considered British rule in India to be a 'sin'. This moral framework was crucial to Gandhi's understanding of and belief in non-violence: 'The world rests upon the bedrock of satya or truth. Asatya, meaning untruth, also means non-existent, and satya or truth also means that which is. If untruth does not so much as exist, its victory is out of the question. And truth being that which is, can never be destroyed. This is the doctrine of satyagraha in a nutshell.'

On the cover of the first edition of his speeches and writings in 1922, Gandhiji printed his credo: 'I believe in loving my enemies. I believe in non-violence as the only remedy . . . I believe in the power of suffering to melt the stoniest heart . . . If the world believes in the existence of a soul, it must be recognized that soul force is better than body force—it is the sacred principle of love which moves mountains.'

Gandhiji was profoundly influenced by the principles of ahimsa and satya and gave both a profound meaning when he applied them to the nationalist cause. This made him the extraordinary leader of the world's first successful non-violent movement for independence from colonial rule. At the same time, he was a philosopher who was constantly seeking to live out his own ideas, whether they applied to individual self-improvement or social change: his autobiography was typically subtitled 'The Story of My Experiments with Truth'. Gandhiji was the first political activist to believe that just ends cannot be attained by unjust means; in satyagraha, means and ends were inseparable.

If truth was his leitmotiv and guiding credo, satyagraha was his principal mode of major action precisely because it was infused with truth, the highest of all moral principles. As he put it elsewhere: 'ahimsa is the means; Truth is the end.'

So non-violence, like many later concepts labelled with a negation, from non-cooperation to non-alignment, meant much more than the denial of an opposite; it did not merely imply the absence of violence. Non-violence was the way to vindicate the truth not by the infliction of suffering on the opponent, but on one's self. In satyagraha, it was essential to willingly accept punishment in order to demonstrate the strength of one's convictions.

Today, in the 'post-truth' era, one can only ask in despair how much of that old spirit of Mahatma Gandhi survives in our country's politics.

43.
Snollygoster

noun

A SHREWD, UNPRINCIPLED POLITICIAN

Though 'Snollygoster' is a fanciful coinage in American English slang going back to 1846, it can easily apply to many practitioners of Indian politics in 2020.

Trust the Americans to come up with a word no one had dreamt of before. Snollygoster (sometimes spelled, less popularly, snallygaster) was originally, in American English, the name of a monster, half-reptile, half-bird, that preyed on both children and chickens—suggesting rural origins. From its usage in 1846 to describe an unprincipled politician, however, it has come to mean 'a rotten person who is driven by greed and self-interest'. That is a description, alas, that in both nineteenth-century USA and twenty-first-century India, more often than not applies to politicians.

In today's US, however, it is often applied to an amoral or inconsiderate boss: 'That old snollygoster who runs this company won't even allow us toilet breaks!' The unusual word indicates a likely German origin, from the immigrant community known as the Pennsylvania Dutch (who were actually German, not Dutch, but since they were Deutsch, the German word for Germans, they became known as Dutch!). The Pennsylvania Dutch had the word schnellegeeschter, 'fast spirits or ghosts', a corruption of the

German schnelleGeister with the same meaning, schnell being fast, and Geist meaning spirit or ghost.

The word enjoyed its vogue in the mid to late nineteenth century, when American politics, in the era of 'robber barons', was dominated by snollygosters associated with New York's Tammany Hall and unscrupulous operators like New York's Boss Tweed. Those were the days when all politicians were assumed to be on the take and available for sale to the highest bidder: it was said of the Rockefellers, who ran Standard Oil, that they did everything for Pennsylvania legislators but refine them.

It is no longer widely used, which is why I decided to resurrect it in a tweet on 27 July 2017, when a chief minister of Bihar, elected alongside Congress and RJD on an anti-BJP platform, suddenly switched sides and joined the BJP. I promptly tweeted: 'Word of the day! *snollygoster* Definition: US dialect: a shrewd, unprincipled politician . . . First Known Use: 1846 . . . Most recent use: 26/7/17.' Of course, I could have resurrected it again when another politician betrayed years of eloquent opposition to the

BJP by joining that party—but it hardly seemed worth repeating, so convinced are Indians that shrewdness and lack of principle are indeed the defining characteristics of Indian politicians.

Snollygoster was reputedly popularized 'almost singlehandedly' by a Georgia Democrat, H.J.W. Ham, who travelled around the US during the 1890s with a stump speech titled 'The Snollygoster in Politics', defining the word as a 'place-hunting demagogue' or a 'political hypocrite'. But Ham was a little too precise in his definition. He said: 'A snollygoster is one with an unquenchable thirst for office with neither the power to get it nor the ability to fill it.'

These days it's hardly employed in the US, where its last recorded use was by the folksy President Truman in 1952. Saying that his grandfather used to tell him that when you heard someone praying loudly in public, 'you had better go home and lock your smokehouse,' Truman denounced Republicans with the term 'snollygosters' as an alternative to describing them as 'bastards' (as he quaintly put it, 'a snollygoster is a man born out of wedlock'). Of course he was immediately corrected by the language mavens of the day, who quoted this splendid definition by an unnamed editor in the *Columbus Dispatch* of Ohio, on 28 October 1895: 'a snollygoster is a fellow who wants office, regardless of party, platform or principles, and who, whenever he wins, gets there by the sheer force of monumental talknophicalassumnacy'. (Don't ask me to explain the last word: it doesn't exist outside this definition.)

Truman continued to use the word: his correspondence with his former Secretary of State, Dean Acheson, reveals Truman lamenting that President Eisenhower had given in to congressional 'snollygosters'—unprincipled politicians.

I prefer the 'shrewd and unprincipled' definition myself, because it is more widely applicable, including to politicians who are indeed able to get the office they cynically aspire to. In our country, alas, where politicians are all too often guided by personal advantage rather than by consistent values, ideological beliefs or moral principles, it is widely believed that to become successful in the world of politics one has to be an accomplished snollygoster.

44.
Spoonerism

noun

A LANGUAGE ERROR INVOLVING
THE SUBSTITUTION OF SYLLABLES OF TWO
WORDS IN CLOSE PROXIMITY TO EACH OTHER

———

USAGE

The preacher Reverend Spooner referred to 'conquering kings' (a phrase from a well-known hymn) as 'Kingering Kongs', thus coining a legendary spoonerism.

This delightful infelicity was the contribution of the nineteenth-century Oxford don and ordained minister Reverend William Archibald Spooner, who unwittingly gave his name to this English-language error, known for a century and a quarter as spoonerisms.

Rev. Spooner was famously absent-minded and tended, in his abstracted way, to switch unintentionally the vowels or consonants in two words in close proximity. Thus, intending to say that 'The rate of wages will press hard upon the employer', the Reverend declared in a lecture that 'The weight of rages will press hard upon the employer'. This and 'Kingering Kongs' are in fact the only substantiated examples authenticated as having been actually uttered by him, but his reputation, enhanced by mischievous Oxford undergraduates who attended his lectures and sermons, spawned an entire cottage industry of invented spoonerisms.

Far from being unintentional mix-ups by an abstracted professor, they were created entirely intentionally for humorous purposes. The most famous, because it was both plausible and hilariously funny, was that in a toast to Queen Victoria, Spooner—instead of raising his glass with the words 'Three cheers for our dear old queen!'—invited those present to give 'Three cheers for our queer old dean!'

Another example has him saying 'The Lord is a shoving leopard' instead of 'The Lord is a loving shepherd'. And asking a couple at a wedding if it was 'customary to kiss' the bride, Spooner is supposed to have said, 'Is it kisstomary to cuss the bride?' In these stories, Spooner renders a 'crushing blow' as a 'blushing crow', calls a well-oiled bicycle a 'well-boiled icicle' and describes a 'cosy little nook' as a 'nosey little cook.'

But in fact most of the famous spoonerisms are apocryphal and cannot be convincingly attributed to him. The Oxford Dictionary of Quotations (third edition, 1979) lists only the 'weight of rages' as a substantiated spoonerism.

The Oxford provenance of most of these invented spoonerisms is apparent in their content. Thus the Reverend, wanting to find out 'Is the Dean busy?', asks 'Is the bean dizzy?' He accuses an undergraduate, 'You were fighting a liar in the quadrangle' as opposed to 'You were lighting a fire in the quadrangle'. Going to church and seeing his customary place in the pew taken, he intends to ask an usher to show him to another seat, but instead says: 'Someone is occupewing my pie. Please sew me to another sheet.' And the most brilliant of all has an indignant Spooner dismissing an errant undergrad from his presence with the words: 'You have hissed all my mystery lectures. You have tasted a whole worm. Please leave Oxford on the next town drain.' ('You have missed all my history lectures. You have wasted a whole term. Please leave Oxford on the next down train.')

The appeal of the spoonerism is that it is a rich source of humour even when it has nothing to do with Oxford or the queer old dean himself. For example: 'I'd rather have a bottle in front of me than a frontal lobotomy.' There's something hilariously accurate about describing a bad 'grilled cheese' sandwich as a 'chilled grease sandwich'. The Washington, D.C. political comedy sketch group Capitol Steps famously referred to President Reagan as 'Resident

Pagan' and described US elections as 'Licking their Peaders' (picking their leaders). The spy wars with Russia were described as the CIA not 'snooping on Putin' but 'poopin' on Snutin'.

That indispensable source of research material, the Internet, tells me that in his poem 'Translation', Brian P. Cleary describes a boy who speaks in spoonerisms (like 'shook a tower' instead of 'took a shower'). Humorously, Cleary leaves the poem's final spoonerism up to the reader when he says: 'He once proclaimed, "Hey, belly jeans" / When he found a stash of jelly beans. / But when he says he "pepped in stew" / We'll tell him he should wipe his shoe.'

45.
Troll

verb and noun

(VERB) 1. TO TRY TO LURE OR INCITE SOMEONE BY PASSING SOMETHING WHERE THEY CAN SEE IT; 2. TO ISSUE HOSTILE OR OFFENSIVE SOCIAL MEDIA POSTS. (NOUN) 1. A NORSE DEMON THAT LIVES UNDER BRIDGES; 2. SOMEONE WHO POSTS PROVOCATIVE MESSAGES TO SOCIAL MEDIA INTENDED TO CAUSE MAXIMUM DISRUPTION

USAGE

The ruling party engages a well-organized army of trolls on social media to attack those of different political views.

The origin of the modern usage of 'troll' is something of a mystery. How a creature from Norse mythology—ugly and slow-witted, dwelling in isolated rocks, mountains, or caves, and often quite hostile to human beings—became emblematic of antisocial behaviour on social media is a mystery, since Norwegians didn't invent Twitter!

In Norse mythology, an ancient tale from the ninth-century book *Skáldskaparmál* describes an encounter between a reciter of heroic verse, Bragi Boddason, and an unnamed troll woman, who aggressively asks him who he is, in the process describing herself. Numerous tales in Scandinavian folklore characterize trolls as very strong, but slow and dim-witted, often man-eaters, and as creatures who turn to stone upon contact with sunlight.

Trolls were always described in these legendary stories as dangerous, given to kidnapping people and overrunning their estates, antisocial and quarrelsome creatures who made life difficult for travellers. Perhaps that explains our modern idea of troll behaviour—it goes back 1100 years!

When the Internet began gaining popularity in the late 1980s and early 1990s, the term used for posting inflammatory or hostile messages was 'flaming', but these 'flamers' soon started being described as 'trolls' instead, and the latter term has completely driven out the former. The troll's intent is usually to insult, offend or abuse his targets in order to provoke a response for the troll's own amusement or to score political points. One definition of 'troll' speaks of online harassment; another is that of 'a person who defaces Internet tribute sites with the aim of causing grief to families'.

Earlier, the non-Internet-related use of 'trolling' occurred in military parlance: there is a 1972 citation from the Vietnam War, in which US Navy pilots spoke of 'trolling for MiGs', meaning using decoys, with the mission of drawing fire away from US planes. This usage has of course been eclipsed by that relating to the Internet, with the *Oxford English Dictionary* finding its earliest usage in this sense in 1992. Here too 'trolling' was a verb, in the phrase 'trolling for newbies', an expression used in alt.folklore.urban (AFU) to refer to questions or topics that had been so repeatedly discussed that only a new user would respond to them earnestly. Such posts would help identify new subscribers. This definition of trolling was relatively benign and meant something much narrower than the contemporary understanding of the term. One of the most famous AFU trollers, David Mikkelson, went on to create the urban folklore website Snopes.com.

From this usage, the noun troll usually referred to an act of trolling—or to the resulting discussion—rather than to the author, though now a troll is always seen as a nasty creature behaving obnoxiously in social media, and 'to troll' is only understood to mean 'to insult, abuse, attack and offend someone on social media through one's posts'. In Kerala politics, however, the word has been transmuted further, and is used (in Malayalam) not to refer to an antisocial individual but to a humorous meme. 'That was a great troll about you!' friends and supporters would tell me gleefully, to my bewilderment, until I realized that words can acquire different meanings in different languages.

There is, in fact, a still older usage of the word 'troll', to mean 'to fish by pulling a line through the water', usually from a slow-moving boat, as opposed to 'trawl', which involves dragging a large net from a much larger boat. In this sense, of course, politicians like myself are always trolling for votes—and that's what our critics, as trolls, do to us on the Internet too!

46.
Umpire

noun

A SPORTING OFFICIAL, ESPECIALLY IN
CRICKET AND ASSOCIATION FOOTBALL,
WHO ADJUDICATES THE GAME

———

USAGE

The umpire ruled him out, even though the evidence for
him having snicked the ball was scanty.

The word 'umpire' has a hoary pedigree. In Middle English, the earliest form of this word is as 'noumper' around 1350 (meaning not a peer, i.e., not a member of one of the teams, and therefore impartial) though it changed to 'umpire' because of a common error. The expression 'a noumper' (with 'a' being the indefinite article) led to a typical confusion also seen elsewhere, with the leading 'n' becoming attached to the article, changing 'a noumper' to 'an oumper' and eventually 'an umpire'. (This kind of linguistic shift, known as 'false splitting', gave us the word 'orange', because of the same mistake in speaking of 'a norange' (the word 'naranj' was the term for the fruit in Arabic, and it initially came to English as 'a norange', only to become 'an orange' because of this false splitting.) The word 'umpire' was applied to the officials of many sports, including football (where it has been superseded by 'referee') and baseball (which still uses it).

In cricket, an umpire is a person who has the authority to make decisions about events on the cricket field, according to the Laws of Cricket, first published in 1774. Besides keeping a record of the number of deliveries bowled and announcing the completion of an over, the umpire makes vital decisions about the legality of the deliveries bowled, appeals for wickets and the general conduct of the game in a legal manner. The umpire is meant to function as a trained professional, knowledgeable in the laws of the game, fully aware of the laws, the relevant match conditions and understanding of the pressures under which the players are playing.

He is required (and expected) to be totally fair and unbiased in the execution of his duties and the making of split-second decisions. The slightest error or misjudgement can transform the course of a match and determine its eventual outcome. As A.G. (Allan) Steel wrote in his chapter on umpiring in the book *Cricket*, written in conjunction with R.H. (Robert) Lyttelton, in 1888: 'If anyone were to ask us the question "What class of useful men receive most abuse and least thanks for their services?" we should, without hesitation, reply, "Cricket umpires." The duties of an umpire are most laborious and irksome; they require for their proper performance the exercise of numerous qualifications, and yet it is always the lot of every man who dons the white coat, the present dress of an umpire, to receive, certainly no thanks, and, too frequently, something which is not altogether unlike abuse.'

A Latin poem by William Goldwin from March 1706 describes two umpires 'leaning on their bats' —apparently in those days the batsmen were required to touch the umpire's bat with theirs to register a run. Over time, of course, this began to be considered somewhat unnecessary, and the umpires' bats were done away with—no doubt saving the umpires a few accidental whacks on their shins by running batsmen.

In the earliest days there were no independent umpires—each side supplied an umpire to ensure an unbiased game was conducted. (This practice persists in much amateur cricket, such as the games I played on weekends as a UN official in Geneva and Singapore.) Subsequently the practice became that the host association (and in Test matches, the host country) supplied the umpires. This resulted in so many outraged cries about biased umpiring that the very viability of international cricket was threatened.

The umpiring bias was real, especially in Pakistan, whose umpires were known to seek instructions from the country's Test captain before a match. During the 1956 MCC tour of Pakistan, several English cricketers brought a particularly egregious Pakistani umpire, Idris Baig, to their room, offered him a drink, and when he asked for water, emptied a couple of buckets of it over him. Baig did not take kindly to this humiliation and the matter snowballed into an international incident, though many a foreign cricketer had probably wished a similar fate upon other Pakistani umpires. (A notable example was Shakoor Rana, with whom the touring English captain, Mike Gatting, had a notorious finger-wagging standoff in 1987.)

By 1986-87 Pakistan's series against the West Indies was played under neutral umpires—as it happens, Indian umpires invited by the Pakistan Cricket Board. Its president, Nur Khan, and skipper Imran had become understandably tired of their team's successes being discredited by the performance of the Pakistani umpires. Their decision to remove allegations of umpiring bias from the equation not only made the cricket tension-free (except for the more enjoyable sporting tensions associated with the run of play), it started a worldwide trend. Today all Tests are umpired by officials from other countries, ODIs feature one host umpire and one neutral, and T20Is two host-country umpires. But one could argue that the introduction of technology has reduced the prospects of bias, since umpiring howlers would be visible on television for the world to see, and the offending umpire's career would plunge more rapidly than an out-of-form batsman's average.

From the traditional two umpires on the field, one standing at the end where the bowler delivers the ball, and one at 90 degrees from the facing batsman (usually, but not always, at square leg), the modern game now uses four umpires: two on-field umpires, a third umpire who watches video replays and adjudicates decisions referred by the on-field umpires, and a fourth umpire who looks after the match balls, takes out the drinks for the umpires and fills in in emergencies.

The International Cricket Council (ICC) has three panels of umpires, an Elite Panel, an International Panel and a Development

Panel. Most Test matches are controlled by members of the Elite Panel, with local members of the International Panel providing support in the third- or fourth-umpire roles. The umpires' old omnipotence has been further undermined in international matches by the creation of a new position of match referee, who enforces the ICC's Cricket Code of Conduct, imposes fines on offending players reported by the umpires, and is tasked with ensuring the game is played in a reputable manner.

Still, the indispensability of the umpire is best summed up in this story of a conversation among three umpires about their craft.

'There's wickets and not-outs,' says the first, 'and I call them as they are.'

'There's wickets and not-outs,' says the second, 'and I call them as I see them.'

The third umpire settles the argument.

'There's wickets and not-outs,' he says, 'but they ain't nothing till I call them.'

47.
Valetudinarian

noun

A PERSON WITH A WEAK OR SICKLY
CONSTITUTION, ESPECIALLY ONE WHOSE
CHIEF CONCERN IS HIS OR HER ILL HEALTH

USAGE

With her litany of complaints about aches and pains, my
friend's grandmother was a valetudinarian, though her
concerns seemed belied by her robust appearance.

I actually once knew a lady like that, a woman of considerable heft, pink-cheeked vigour and strength of voice, whose only conversation seemed to be about her alarmingly poor health, which was apparent to no one but herself. Everyone humoured her lamentations, thinking them to be reflective of a harmless hypochondria, until, to everyone's general astonishment, she passed away in her sleep one night without having exhibited the slightest symptom of the maladies she was constantly complaining about.

Indian society seems full of valetudinarians, not least because health is such a popular subject of conversation. Everyone has home remedies to suggest and miracle cures to offer for your slightest affliction, which seems to bring out the self-pity in all of us. We are all amateur doctors, and every bit of medical advice gets a receptive audience, because every one of us is at heart a valetudinarian!

The word itself comes from the Latin *valetudinarius*, and connotes someone unduly anxious about his health. Sometimes it's a polite way of saying hypochondriac, and it has a long pedigree: an article in the *Gentleman's Magazine* in London in 1787 remarked that: 'Everyone knows how hard a task it is to cure a valetudinarian.' (An echo of the lovely Indian proverb that reminds us how hard it is to wake a man who is pretending to sleep.) A valetudinarian is constantly wallowing in the narcissism of his own ill-health.

That can't be a pleasant place to be. The American polymath and President, Thomas Jefferson, wisely observed, 'The most uninformed mind, with a healthy body, is happier than the wisest valetudinarian.'

48.
Vigilante

noun

A MEMBER OF A SELF-APPOINTED GROUP OF
CITIZENS WHO UNDERTAKE LAW ENFORCEMENT
ACTIONS WITHOUT LEGAL AUTHORITY, OFTEN
INVOLVING PHYSICAL VIOLENCE AGAINST AN
ACCUSED OR SUSPECTED LAW-BREAKER

———

USAGE

The gau-rakshak samitis have constituted themselves into
vigilante groups, intercepting and assaulting anyone they
suspect to be transporting cattle illegally for slaughter.

Though the word vigilante derives in the first place from the Spanish word for 'watchman', by the mid-nineteenth century its usage in American English referred to a 'member of a vigilance committee' set up by communities to reinforce policing actions in the Wild West. Both words derive in turn from the Latin *vigilantem*, meaning 'watchful, anxious, careful', as does the English word vigil—to keep vigil is to be watchful and awake for signs of danger or intrusion. Vigilance committees kept informal, if rather rough, law and order going on the expanding US western frontier and in similar places where official authority had not been fully established. A vigilante served such a committee in the belief that he was serving the security interests of his community.

Since law and order has been pretty much formally established everywhere by now, why do vigilantes still exist? Vigilantes often justify themselves, or rationalize their roles, by arguing that too often the formal mechanisms of law enforcement aren't doing their jobs properly. In their telling, official legal forms of criminal punishment are either insufficient or inefficient. Vigilantes normally see the government as incapable of enforcing the law; in India they often claim the police are either corrupt or not energetic enough to tackle crimes like cow slaughter, so they feel a 'moral obligation' to take the law into their own hands. The vigilantes justify what they are doing as fulfilling the wishes of the community, which the police have been either unwilling or unable to do.

As we know all too well from the recent flare-up of vigilantism in northern India, vigilante conduct involves varied degrees of violence. Vigilantes tend to assault their targets both verbally and physically, vandalize their property, and beat or even murder individuals. People accused of crimes that carry high emotional resonance with the vigilantes, especially those involving cow protection or assaults on women, are often punished by vigilantes to general public approval.

There are many problems with vigilantism, the most obvious of which is the denial of an opportunity for a suspect to prove his innocence. The vigilante goes after an accused without any of the niceties of the genuine law-enforcement officer; no rights are read to the target, nor is he given a chance to explain his innocence. Vigilantism has often involved targets being killed or irreversibly damaged on the basis of mistaken identities. People wrongly accused of rape or theft, or of trafficking in children or slaughtering cows, have been the particular target of vigilantism in India since 2014. This is why most people think the actions of the vigilante are often worse than the original crime he claims to be avenging.

Vigilantism strikes the modern mind as wrong and unacceptable, but it is not always frowned upon by the communities on whose behalf it is conducted. Folklore and legend are full of tales of vigilante justice told with great approbation, since in these tales the vigilante challenges the amorality of the official order to redress injustice. When legitimate authority is either weak or tyrannical and the formal apparatus of governance is ethically inadequate, many ask, why shouldn't a vigilante step in to restore justice? After all, Robin Hood was at bottom a vigilante.

The answer lies, of course, in strengthening the official apparatus of law-enforcement and justice, streamlining and speeding up the judicial system and strengthening the institutions of governance so the public will have their faith in the official system restored—not in giving a free rein to vigilantes to take the law into their own hands, thus shaming us all. Today's vigilante is no modern Robin Hood, but just a hood robbing us of our dignity and rights.

49.
Whistleblower

noun

SOMEONE WHO REPORTS ILLEGAL, UNETHICAL OR INAPPROPRIATE ACTIVITIES IN AN ORGANIZATION, COMPANY OR GOVERNMENT DEPARTMENT

USAGE

The corrupt official denounced the whistleblower as a tattle-tale, a snitch, a squealer, and a stool pigeon, but once the judge had heard the whistleblower's facts, the official still ended up in jail.

Whistleblower is an evocative word; it immediately conjures up an image of a stern football referee blowing the whistle on some infraction, and that's precisely what a whistleblower does. He (or she) is a figure of rectitude, someone who has witnessed wrongdoing from the inside and cannot abide it. Whistleblowers are the bane of those who break laws and rules: since most of the crimes they reveal are committed in secret, their testimony is indispensable to uncovering them.

The moral dilemma that confronts a whistleblower is that of his own complicity: as an insider in the organization where he finds a wrong being committed, he has a choice between staying loyal or blowing the whistle. Sometimes whistleblowers have been involved in the wrongs they reveal but reach a point when they cannot take any more. Sometimes their accidental or unauthorized discovery of a crime they were no part of, and of which they disapprove, makes them whistleblowers.

There are few things that can stop a sincerely motivated whistleblower. Governments have the Official Secrets Act or the equivalent which prohibit employees from revealing secret information they may come across in the course of their work.

Some companies, especially large corporations, have a non-disparagement clause in their employment contracts to discourage whistleblowing. But these only deter the timid, the intimidated or those with inactive consciences (who tell themselves they need the salary or the job more than the world needs to know about their boss's illegal activities).

Especially with the passage of whistleblower protection laws in most democracies, including ours, such considerations have rarely prevented whistleblowing. It was a whistleblower, listening in on an official phone call to take notes, who revealed President Trump's misuse of his power for his personal political ends. An Indian whistleblower revealed the fudging of pharmaceutical research data in Ranbaxy, practically destroying the company.

The phrase is said to have been invented by American civic activist Ralph Nader, but etymologists say it goes back to the nineteenth century and he should only be credited with bringing it into modern popular use. The word was linked to the conduct of US and British police and law enforcement officials in the nineteenth century, who used a whistle to warn a fugitive, alert the public or summon additional police.

The usage of the word has also evolved over time. An 1883 American newspaper story called a policeman who used his whistle to alert citizens about a riot a whistle blower (two words). Eight decades later, the two-word phrase had become a single hyphenated word, whistle-blower. With its popularization by Nader and the American media in the 1960s as a respectable term for people who revealed wrongdoing, it became the compound word whistleblower.

A whistleblower can choose to blow the whistle by revealing information or allegations either internally or externally. Internally, a whistleblower can bring the wrongdoing he discovers to the attention of senior people within the same organization who he believes are not complicit. Sometimes corporations or government departments may have an officer assigned to receive internal whistleblower complaints. Alternatively, a whistleblower can bring allegations to light by contacting an outsider—often the media but also, in government, another official, or if a straightforward crime is involved, police or law enforcement.

Whistleblowing is not a risk-free activity: it can cost you your job, and if your identity is revealed to the accused, result in reprisal actions against you and punitive retaliation: lawsuits, criminal charges, social stigma and job termination are all possible consequences. This would almost certainly be the case in most private companies; in government, a whistleblower is protected by law, but no private company is going to retain an employee, however moral, who has betrayed a confidence and lost his employer's trust.

From a company's point of view, whistleblowing is unethical for breaching confidentiality, especially in businesses that handle sensitive client or patient information. This is why most private company employees keep their head down when they discover their employer is breaking the law; at best, if their consciences are affronted, they set about looking for another job. A morally upright whistleblower, therefore, is a rarity, and for that reason must be hailed as a hero.

50.
Xenophobia

noun

FEAR OR HATRED OF ANYTHING OR
ANYONE ALIEN OR FOREIGN

———

USAGE

It's difficult to tell if exercises like the National Register
of Citizens are motivated by xenophobia or mere politics.

The fear of foreigners is, of course, neither new nor particularly Indian, but the word for it is only a century and a quarter old. It seems to have been coined in the UK in the late nineteenth century—with an 1880 citation from a London newspaper the earliest one etymologists can find—from two Greek roots, *xeno-* (meaning 'foreign, strange') and *-phobia* (meaning 'fear'). The adjective formed from it is xenophobic. The modern Greek tourist industry likes to tout that Greeks speak a language that does not differentiate between 'foreigner' and 'guest', for 'xenos' can be used for both those terms.

That first citation contrasts xenophobia with another late-nineteenth-century coinage, xenomania ('an inordinate attachment to foreign things'), but that word—and the taste it describes—has not had the same staying power as its antonym. The London newspaper I cited earlier dismissed xenophobia as 'always unintelligent', but Americans and other Europeans have been somewhat more receptive. The fear of foreigners invading the States was not unreasonable, given that that was how the country was established in the first place. Today, it crops up more in relation to the dislike of immigrants, with the hostility expressed by Trump supporters in the 2016 elections being matched by the xenophobic rhetoric around Brexit in the UK (directed principally at East Europeans flocking in under EU rules) and the invective of Marine Le Pen and other xenophobes in West European politics. Even in India, it is the passions raised by the issue of alleged illegal immigration from Bangladesh that has led to talk of xenophobia, and it is in that context that it is used most commonly these days in India.

Xenophobia is the fear or hatred of that which one perceives as foreign or strange or at minimum unfamiliar. Xenophobia usually involves people in a position of dominance in a society or country reacting with suspicion towards the activities of others, usually minorities, immigrants, outsiders or 'aliens' in some sense, whose presence or growth, it is feared, could cause a dilution or loss of national, ethnic or racial identity. Xenophobia gets dangerous when it translates to a desire to eliminate the presence of these outsiders in order to secure the country's (or dominant group's) presumed purity.

Xenophobia is not merely prejudice towards foreigners: it can also involve the uncritical exaltation of one's own culture, in which one exaggerates to an unreal, stereotyped and extreme extent the quality of the culture one is seeking to protect. According to UNESCO, which defines xenophobia as 'an attitudinal orientation of hostility against non-natives in a given population', xenophobia and racism often overlap, but this is not necessarily so: the Nazis were xenophobes and racists, as are many of the anti-immigrant politicians in Europe, but Indians who favour citizenship for Bengali Hindus but not Bengali Muslims can hardly be accused of racism, since both groups belong to the same 'race' and ethnicity.

History is replete with examples of xenophobia, from the Ancient Greeks denigrating foreigners as 'barbarians', to the Chinese feeling the same way about foreigners a millennia and a half later, all the way to President Trump declaring that the US is the greatest country on earth and vowing to keep Muslims out of it.

In the contemporary world, xenophobia arises in many societies, and particularly in democracies, when people feel that their rights to benefit from the government's programmes, welfare benefits and job opportunities are being encroached upon by other people. By declaring these others to be less entitled to the benefits that are your right, the xenophobe provides a basis for discrimination against the outsider.

In the 1990s, xenophobic outbursts were followed by an increase in acts of racist violence in several societies in the world. This rise of xenophobia led UNESCO to theorize about a 'new racism' that developed in the post-war era, since racism no longer was based on biological but rather on cultural differences.

Two causes are put forward by theorists to explain the recent resurgence of xenophobic and racist movements. One is the new migration patterns that have developed as an effect of the gradual internationalization of the labour market during the post-colonial era. In the receiving countries, social groups in unfavourable positions in their societies resented newcomers as competitors for jobs and public services. This cultivated a social and political climate that generated xenophobia and racism (defensive reactions against migrants), as well as nationalism (demands that the state provide better protection against foreigners for its own population).

The second cause believed to reinforce xenophobia and racism is the backlash against globalization, which has led states to reduce their social welfare, education and healthcare services in many developed countries. This reduction influenced in particular the segments of the population living on the margins of society. These groups are often in direct competition with migrants for such services and are the main breeding ground for xenophobia and racism. Research has shown that those perceived to be outsiders or foreigners—usually migrants, refugees, asylum-seekers, displaced persons and those who cannot prove their nationality—are the main targets of those suffering from economic inequalities and marginalization. Their social decline can be exploited by right-wing political organizations through xenophobic ideologies.

Unfortunately, countering xenophobia requires leadership from the government to resist it by exhortation and by example. But when a government itself is complicit in whipping up xenophobia, a society is forced to call on its own highest values to resist succumbing to it.

This is where we in India find ourselves today.

51.
Yogi

noun

A PRACTITIONER OF YOGA, A PERSON WHO
IS AN AUTHORITY ON YOGA, HAS PRACTISED
YOGA AND ATTAINED A HIGHER LEVEL OF
CONSCIOUSNESS

———

USAGE

The Beatles became devotees of Maharishi Mahesh Yogi,
who had translated his knowledge of yogic practices into a
new science of 'Transcendental Meditation'.

The English word yogi comes, of course, from the Hindi योगी (yogī), which in turn is derived from the Sanskrit योगिन् (yogin), which descends from the verbal root yuj, coming from युनक्ति (yunakti), to connect. In Hinduism, the god Lord Shiva and his consort, the goddess Parvati, are often depicted as an emblematic yogi–yogini pair. It must be admitted, however, that in the West, the word 'yogi' became popular from the cartoon character, Yogi Bear, who was known for conning tourists out of their picnics—a far cry from the Indian yogi's meditative practices based on profound religious and spiritual training.

Though the earliest evidence of yogis and their spiritual tradition is found in the *Kesin* hymn 10.136 of the *Rig Veda*, which is as old a Hindu tradition as it is possible to get, the term yogin also appears in the *Katyayana Shrauta-sutra* and in Chapter 6 of the *Maitri Upanishad*, where it means 'a follower of the Yoga system, a contemplative saint'. The term also sometimes refers to a person who belongs to the Natha tradition.

While the term yogi clearly has a very specific meaning, it can, by extension, be applied to people who demonstrate the qualities of yogis without necessarily being trained in yoga or meditative practices. I remember describing my old boss, United Nations Secretary-General Kofi Annan, as someone who was 'anchored in himself like a yogi', immune to either pleasure or pressure, able to focus on the challenges before him with serene detachment. To the best of my knowledge, he had never practised yoga, but was rather a Wise Man in the African tradition, someone who practised these virtues as hallmarks of personal character rather than as the fruits of a spiritual or religious system.

Yogi Bear is a totally different phenomenon, and I remain at a loss at to why his creators dreamt up his first name, since the avaricious bear in question displays not a single yogic quality. Nor does the other famous American 'Yogi', the baseball player Yogi Berra, who no doubt acquired his monicker only because of the similarity of his Italian-derived surname to that of the eponymous Bear. Still, this has led many Americans to be bemused by the term, precisely because they associate it with a cartoon bear and a baseballer rather than with any otherworldly spiritual wisdom.

On the other hand, we in India have the chief minister of Uttar Pradesh, Ajay Bisht, who chooses to go by the name 'Yogi Adityanath'. From his sponsorship of the rough-and-ready 'Hindu Vahini' to his propensity for proposing changes to the names of towns across the country, there seems nothing remotely yogi-like about Mr Bisht. Still, it is one of the anomalies of the Hindu faith that there is no single recognized spiritual body to award official certificates of yogi-hood. Various bodies award the title of yogi, for people of varying qualifications and spiritual merit. At the end of the day, all that matters, if you want to be a yogi, is the number of people who are prepared to take you at your word, and accept you as one.

52.
Zealot

noun

A PERSON WHO IS UNCOMPROMISING
AND OFTEN FANATICAL IN PURSUIT OF HIS
RELIGIOUS CONVICTIONS, POLITICAL BELIEFS,
OR OTHER IDEALS

USAGE

Arguing with a zealot is futile; it is like trying
to read a newspaper in a high wind.

The term zealot is now used only metaphorically, but it is derived from a real group of people who actually existed in recorded history. The Zealots—the term is derived from the Greek *zelotes*, meaning 'emulator, zealous admirer or follower'—were members of an ancient Jewish sect, founded by Judas of Galilee in first-century Judea, who were fanatically devoted to the idea of a world Jewish theocracy. They conducted a fierce resistance against the Romans and sought to expel them from the Holy Land by force, most notably during the First Jewish–Roman War (AD 66–70), which ended badly for the Zealots with the destruction of Herod's Temple and of Jerusalem itself. Their founder paid a high price for his beliefs: two of Judas' sons, Jacob and Simon, were executed by the Romans for their involvement in a revolt.

The Zealots habitually fought to the death and were implacable in their beliefs, including being ruthless with any fellow Jews they believed to be collaborating with the hated Roman Empire, executing or severely persecuting any they could find. Josephus wrote of a murderous 'reign of terror' against Jewish apostates and those who wished to live in peace. Zealots resorted to terrorism and assassination and became known as Sicarii or 'dagger men', lurking in public places with hidden daggers to kill people they considered too friendly to Rome.

Zealotry was not just a term for their cause but was even considered a fourth school of Jewish philosophy by the historian Josephus. They had 'an inviolable attachment to liberty,' he wrote, 'and say that God is to be their only Ruler and Lord.' Simon the Zealot was listed among the apostles selected by Jesus in the Gospel of Luke and in the Acts of the Apostles.

Most Jews did not regard the Zealots very highly: they were largely condemned for their blind fanaticism and congenital aggression, their unwillingness to compromise, and their refusal to agree to peace treaties negotiated by the rabbis to save besieged Jerusalem (they preferred to fight on even knowing that death was certain). In the Talmud, the Zealots are described as irreligious and also as 'boorish', 'wild', or 'ruffians', and are condemned for their aggression and blind militarism. (The Zealots even destroyed decades' worth of food supplies and stocks of firewood in besieged Jerusalem to leave the resident Jews no choice but to fight the Romans out of desperation.) Many blamed them for forcing a civil war within the Jewish community that ensured the Roman victory.

The fate of their modern-day descendants is no better; nobody likes a zealot. The term is always uncomplimentary in its usage, meant to denote an unreasoning fanatic who not only refuses to entertain contrary views but is so convinced of the rightness of his beliefs that he tries to convert you to his way of thinking. While zealots are always passionate, fervent and ardent, filled with intense enthusiasm for their convictions, like their historical forebears their zeal is not always matched by good judgement.

In its broadest usage the term can apply these days to anyone who is almost religiously devoted to a belief, an ideal, a cause, a culture, a person, a way of life or even an object. Most football fans, and all football hooligans, are zealots for their teams. Most good diplomats are not. That master of diplomacy, the eighteenth-century French statesman Talleyrand, famously admonished his young trainees:

'*surtout, pas trop de zèle*' ('above all, not too much zeal'). After all, too much zeal signifies an unwillingness to listen to the other person's point of view—and what could be a worse failing in a diplomat?

53.
Zugzwang

noun

IN CHESS AND OTHER GAMES,
A 'COMPULSION TO MOVE' THAT
PLACES THE MOVER AT A DISADVANTAGE

———

USAGE

The grandmaster, outwitted by his opponent, found
himself in zugzwang and chose to resign.

Zugzwang, a word of German origin, comes from two German roots, *Zug* (move) and *Zwang* (compulsion), so that zugzwang means 'being forced to make a move'. It refers to a situation often found in chess (and sometimes in other board games) in which the player finds himself at a disadvantage because he is forced to make a move that will have adverse consequences for his position in the game. Zugzwang applies particularly in those situations where the rules of the game do not permit one to simply pass and decline to move. In zugzwang, the player being compelled to move always means that their move will create a significantly weaker position for them in the game. A player is said to be 'in zugzwang' when any possible move will make their situation worse—but they have no choice but to do it even if it leads to certain defeat.

Although the term emerges from games such as chess, it is also used in combinatorial game theory to denote a move that directly changes the outcome of the game, turning it from a win to a loss. This is why I found it appropriate to recall the word when the Maharashtra political crisis of 2019 reached its climax and the three-day government of Devendra Fadnavis and Ajit Pawar was forced to resign. When they were sworn in in a 'midnight coup' in the wee hours of a winter Saturday, it looked like the BJP had pulled a fast one on their rivals, the Shiv-Sena-NCP-Congress combine that had been spending several weeks putting together a coalition government for the state. The adroit manoeuvring of NCP supremo Sharad Pawar, the resort to 'resorts' that placed vulnerable legislators of the three parties out of the reach of BJP poachers, and the decision of the Supreme Court forcing a confidence vote on 27 November, placed the short-lived government in zugzwang. Fadnavis and Ajit Pawar had no choice but to resign. Their triumph had turned into a fiasco.

The tables were turned in Madhya Pradesh a few months later, when the BJP placed Congress Chief Minister Kamal Nath in zugzwang. First, by packing off twenty-two MLAs to a resort in Bangalore, they deprived him of the opportunity to persuade them to change their minds. Then, by prolonging the Parliament session in Delhi despite the coronavirus outbreak, they prevented him from using the COVID-19 crisis to suspend or defer the legislative session and so buy time. Finally, the chief minister, acknowledging the reality of his diminished numbers and the unavoidability of a confidence vote he was doomed to lose, resigned.

The term zugzwang was first used in German chess literature in the mid-nineteenth century, and seems to have passed into the English language when it was used as such by chess World Champion Emanuel Lasker in 1905. Indians, however, knew of the concept of zugzwang in our writings about the ancient Indian game of chaturaṅga (later Persianized as shatranj) dating back to the early ninth century, though I have been unable to trace the Sanskrit equivalent of the term, which now seems to have lost out to its upstart German version, even if that was invented a thousand years later. In early Indian chaturanga (c. 500–700), the king could be captured and this ended the game; this was when compulsory moves left the opponent in zugzwang. (The Persian form of the game later introduced the checkmate concept, so the king could not be captured, and zugzwang merely resulted in resignation.)

The earliest written reference to zugzwang found so far occurs in writings on shatranj by Zairab Katai, published sometime between 813 and 833, more than a millennium ago!

Positions with zugzwang occur fairly often in chess endgames, especially in king and pawn endgames. 'Putting the opponent in zugzwang is a common way to help the superior side win a game,' says one chess source, 'and in some cases, it is necessary in order to make the win possible.' One could very well apply that lesson to Maharashtra or in Madhya Pradesh.

In fact when the Fadnavis/Ajit Pawar swearing-in occurred, I had first dusted off another word from my lexicon on Twitter, recalling 'snollygoster', an 1845 American coinage for a 'shrewd, unprincipled politician'. But once the swearing-in turned into a swearing-at, a new word seemed apposite. After all, the coalition had not actually yet staked their claim to form a government. It was the position of their opponents in zugzwang that finally made their win possible.